THE 21ST CENTURY CRISES:

How You Can Thrive In The Virtual Planet

By: Samuel Adeosun

Table of Contents

Fore**word**

In this timely classic, Samuel Adeosun shares profound and crystal information that paints a true picture of what our rapidly changing world has come to be. However, the conversation does not start and end there, it goes on to unfold before the reader's eye what the requisite paradigms, skills, and mode of engagement should become.

The reality that our planet is fast evolving from a traditional physical world to a connected stream of 1s and 0s is immediately brought to bear. Given the current scheme of events, the COVID-19 Lockdowns, new variants of the virus, vaccination, and tracking, the world as we know it is about to morph into something completely novel.

The well-curated information and accurate statistics in the opening chapters of the book help put the reader's mind in proper perspective, which shows readiness for what is coming next both in the world as a whole and in the subsequent chapters of the book (zeugma intended).

The Author goes on an intellectual discourse by starting with the problem statement – the reality of the current crisis. He goes on to help the reader see the different kinds of changes, the external, the internal, and the ones where we are the causative agents.

The striking feature of the conversation is the subliminal message of optimism that is being propagated as refined knowledge is offered, hence the right attitude adjustments are being inspired.

Adjustment, alongside a clear understanding of how the new scheme of things holds and also at the same time, reveals both the ecosystem and requisite skills for thriving.

In all, this material you have in your hands is not just some book, but a roadmap to get you from where you are to a vantage position as the future catches you.

John Nnamaka

Executive Strategist, RExI

Introduction

Hello Dear Friend, I am glad this life-changing book is in your hands. The truth is, I prayed for you to have it even though I don't know your name or where you are reading from. But trust me, your life is about to experience an exponential shift. With this book in your hands, I can boldly say that you now have the answer you have been in search of to live a much better life. All you have to do is to make the right choice to finish reading this book and take bold steps on whatever it is you'll learn.

Ponder These Realities With Me!

What will you do when you suddenly realize the entire world is in total lockdown again? How will you feel when the world you have known for decades is caught up in the shadows of one of the greatest crises it has ever experienced? How will you prepare for the unforeseen circumstances you will encounter in life and what will be your recovery strategies when life smacks you down unprepared?

Economically, what would be your response to a **total blackout** after a lifetime of hard work, dedication, commitment, and loyalty to a chosen career, religion, relationship, and wealth amassing? What will you do when a lifelong dream and investment is suddenly taken from you because of a global, or personal crisis, new demands, and skills in the market space?

How will you bounce back after institutions like the World Health Organization (WHO), United Nations (UN), the developed countries, and advanced economies that were expected to offer solutions to a pandemic or financial crisis suddenly announce to you that they have no answer to the world's most challenging problems?

For instance, the **International Monetary Fund (IMF)'s World Economic Outlook Update**, titled "**A Crisis Like No Other, An Uncertain Recovery**" states that "out of the approximately 2 billion informally employed workers worldwide, the International Labor Organization estimates that close to 80 percent have been significantly affected."

In the article – "**4 Ways Digitization Can Unlock Africa's Recovery**," Joakim Reiter wrote 'The full human cost of COVID-19 in Africa is not yet known, but it is going to be significant.'

The **economies** of most of the developing countries and some parts of South Asia are in **shambles**. The GDPs (Gross Domestic Product) of these countries are in the negative and it seems there is no way out because of its devastating nature. What a global calamity!

Moving forward as a parent in this recession, how will you surmount the courage to tell your family you can no longer fulfill their expectations as far as security, support, and provision is concerned, because of a major and unforeseen crisis? How will you get your children educated when the educational system of your country is failing? Tell me, how?

Or where will you go when it finally dawns on you that your skills are no more needed in the marketplace and your place of work? How will you ask the family you once left to accept you back the moment you realize the future you were preparing for has suddenly disappeared or been swept off by an unknown force, like COVID-19, and recession or scarcity?

Critically, where will you go when the ones you seek help from are helpless, and also in search of answers? What will you do when it seems as if the world powers, global elites, stakeholders, and renowned scientific and research minds, seem not to have a solution to the cause of COVID-19, unforeseen wars, and other major crises that makes you think; "Could this be the end of the world?"

In tandem with the hardship, uncertainties, joblessness, and pressure in the world today, what is your master plan to live the fulfilled life you have always dreamt of? How do you plan to multiply your current stream of income and be at the top of the turbulence in the world? Do you even have any plans to contribute to your society and the global village? Are you giving up and giving in already? Or are you looking for a way out to remain significant even after your exit on earth?

My dear, all the above questions are the real situations of our current habitation. And if you as an individual don't find answers to them, you might never recover from the crisis that has befallen planet Earth and the subsequent crises we will encounter.

Interestingly enough, the United States reports from the BBC and CNN that more than 30 million Americans have lost their jobs as of May 2020! So, everyone, not the government alone, needs to put on their thinking caps and ask: Where are we and where are we going from here? What should be our priorities in this season for relevance and sustainability? **Who has the answer?**

You see, I know we all encounter situations over which we have no personal control, or have the ability to foreclose. And perhaps, many of us are still trying to recuperate from our crises before the crises of COVID, WAR & RECESSION hit us. Well, this isn't the time for depression, accepting defeats, casting blame, regrets, feeling sorry, guilty, and entertaining suicidal thoughts. Instead, it is time to prepare for what's ahead. Covid-19 and scarcity have happened, and the Russia-Ukraine war is now on its 183rd day. It's like the list is increasing. Well, these events have ushered the world into all kinds of global crises, witty innovations, and inventions. And the truth is that there's nothing you can do about it. What you need now is to live with this reality, brace up and look for means to become the answer in your community.

On this note, you must come to understand that living on earth requires that you expect the unexpected and prepare for the unforeseen. It is interestingly part of nature, and of course, the beauty of life. You can't hide or run away from it. But it's quite unfortunate that many of us have not been taught how to build the necessary mental, emotional, psychological, and spiritual capacities to successfully and effectively see opportunities in these kinds of situations and navigate our way through them to victory.

Dear friend, I want you to know that this book is for you and your generation. It is a book designed to help you survive and remain significant in any form of crisis. Whether the crisis is self-induced or externally motivated. Strategies and ideas that would help you rebound and shine are documented for you in this book. This book is written to help you survive in the current and future crises by conserving the resources you have (especially money), multiply them, and as well, adequately prepare you for the new demands and skills in the digital market space.

"Diamonds are just charcoal

*that has handled the **crisis** of heat
exceptionally well.*

Now, the question is;

Will you handle this global

crisis [and others in the future]

in an exceptional way?"

- Samuel **Adeosun**

CHAPTER **ONE**

The 21st Century Crises

Have you ever imagined a world without movements and physical interactions? A world filled with robots or permit me to say humanoids with body shapes built to resemble the human physical structure, designed to carry out some selective human operations powered by Narrow AI (Artificial Intelligence) algorithms and programs - *A world where humanoids and humans coexist. As professor Richard Baldwin suggested, a workplace where humans and machines [robots] work side by side.*

Moving forward, imagine a world where more complex and sophisticated devices are becoming implantable within the human body to combat any kind of disease, enhance sensual cognition and as well, provide entertainment or communication in a way the world has never seen before. This is one of the goals of Tesla CEO, Elon Musk, with one of his companies, called 'Neuralinks.'

Imagine a world where you wouldn't have to carry tangible or physical monies with you anymore but make use of digital monies or currency for transactions. Amazing right? Not too long ago, I watched a newsreel on **China Global Television Network, CGTN**. It was titled **"China's Eye on Block-chain"**. It showed how China and other countries are preparing for digital currencies and using blockchain technology to drive digital currencies, globally.

Let's now Imagine a world where people attend wedding ceremonies, dinner and birthday parties, conferences, seminars, interviews, et al with the aid of a hologram; a three-dimensional projection, which can be seen without using any special equipment such as cameras or glasses. What will it look like?

A world of Virtual Reality (VR): a three-dimensional and computer-designed environment that can be explored by a person. A world where the person becomes part of the virtual or spatial world and he's able to perform a series of actions with the aid of headsets, and special gloves to create any kind of reality he or she wants. A world of driverless and flying cars or road-able aircraft that provides door-to-door transportation by air and by roads. Simply put, a magical world made possible by scientific or technological ingenuity!

Scientifically, we are now entering the **hospital of the future.** A world where smart toilets can monitor your health by analyzing your body fluids three times a day just to detect proteins from cancer colonies. A world where cancer and some deadly diseases would no longer coexist with the human body because of the smart toilets' ability to predict your health status in years to come in a bid to orientate you on how to effectively care for your body system.

It is a world you can grow your skins, blood, heart valves, blood vessels, bones, noses, and ears from your cells. A future where livers, windpipes, and pancreas can be easily adjusted and worked on via technologies.

Well, I am glad to inform you that we are already in that world - dispensation. A world that continues to birth many weird inventions, surprises, shocks, and tragically the COVID-19 crisis that everyone has accepted to live with just like Malaria and cancer. Take, for instance, the likes of AI, 3-D printing, quantum technology, 5G technology, robotics, CRISPR Cas9, etc., which are now as real as anything in this world. A world that opens you up to the possibilities of heightened creative thinking, innovative prowess, and the potential of achieving groundbreaking achievements. Can I be sincere with you?

Nothing! I mean nothing can stop these **'technological miracles'** from becoming integral parts of our existence; until the end of space-time (conscious and matter existence)! All of this will affect our socioeconomic and religious institutions, businesses, politics, values, relations, education, and others.

On this note, if you're not well informed and prepared for what's ahead, chances are that you might not come out of these miracles a victor. You might become obsolete and irrelevant. If you're still part of the masses who think the pandemic and the technological innovations would be over soon and we'll go back to our previous world, I am sorry to announce to you that, you're nothing but a victim of this COVID-19-induced and Fourth Industrial Revolution (4IR) transformation.

The truth might a bitter pill to swallow. However, the truth must be told. It's a reality that has come to stay. The smartest and bravest thing I require from you is to accept all these and be ready to navigate and position yourself well to ride the current, uncertain, and turbulent future ahead of us. **The world has changed forever!**

In actual fact, Prof. Richard Baldwin puts it poignantly and clearly in one of his numerous talks on AI, robotics, globalization, economy, automation, the jobs of the future, the workplace, professions of the future, and our emerging new world after the coronavirus pandemic, etc. that;

In 'Globalization, Robotics, and the Future of Work', he said thus 'The transformation that automation, artificial intelligence, and robotics brings is already changing our lives - but the oncoming digital tsunami will be much more powerful than we realize.'

Hence, it's no longer news that the world is in crisis. At some point in time, the world experienced a total lockdown because of the lethal disease called COVID-19. In short, the global market and leadership are still experiencing the effects of this disease. Countries and territories around the world have taken different approaches to tackle the effects of the lockdown. The World Health Organization recommended curfews and lockdowns be short-term to assess how to reorganize, rebalance resources and protect health services just like business experts are putting heads together for a solution around the recession.

The effects of this virus have influenced structures like churches, mosques, gardens, cafeterias, super or mini markets, and all public gatherings are massive. It influenced our movements, international trade and commerce, immigration and migration, cultural interactions/relationships, and many more to a high degree. Thus, the need for new approaches and ideologies on how to live, and continue our daily activities. Of course, ideas on how to reset and scale through to become better in this trying and tragic time and beyond are much needed. The reason you must take responsibility. Because everyone, including the elite, experts, and global leaders is all confused and looking for a way out. It's a blow and a shock to humankind as a whole.

According to a **newsreel by Al Jazeera English**, it states in **'How will the**

Global Economy Ever Recover from the Coronavirus?' thus "The global economy is shutting down because of COVID-19. Many millions of people are without work and struggling." That is the extent to which the pandemic has affected the world economy and disrupted the existing order across the world.

Every country in the world is currently experiencing some kind of difficulty; some, like the U.S., have entered into a recession or as Prof. Paul Krugman (Nobel laureate) and others argue, are rapidly moving into an 'Economic Depression' worse than those of the 1930s! Unemployment rates are zooming. Particularly in developing countries, low-income countries, or third-world countries like Nigeria.

Today, unemployment, famine, insecurity, rape, fear, depression, and deaths have become the order of the day. The world's economy is crumbling.

Fear and depression are everywhere. People are constantly in search of alternatives. All kinds of Ponzi schemes and other criminal activities have risen tremendously. Ultimately, only God can help us! We need a divine intervention at the material time in our history!

In the global world today, it is now obvious that everyone is going through this crisis together. And the truth is that most of us are (or will soon be) experiencing personal crises which will be directly or indirectly related to the broader crisis in the world. As the WHO (World Health Organization), financial institutions, and other health-related agencies have been sensitizing and trying to inform us ahead, we need to take heed and prepare our minds for what's ahead. It seems we are coming back to the pre-Covid-19 era, but the truth is, we are not. So, get ready.

Technological futurists, global leaders, and experts in different fields, i.e. Bill Gates, Jack Dorsey (CEO of Twitter), etc. keep stressing the need to explore digital platforms like online space and channels, going forward. In other words, you might lose your job in the coming months or years if you don't know how to maneuver your way around the digital space.

It is important to emphasize, at this juncture, that with some digital skills, curiosity, and Internet-enabled device(s) i.e. laptop or smartphone, one can easily get an online job that pays well in America, Nigeria, or any part of the world. Payment could be done via Paystack, PayPal, Money Gram, Western Union, and the likes.

Also, job opportunities have left the traditional walls of physical buildings, most jobs are now done in space; the new digital ecosystem. For example, if you own a business, you may have to pull back to rethink and come up with new strategies for making it through this hard season. You need to be in the cloud or cyberspace to at least meet your potential customers.

If you are a pastor or a missionary and all your trust is in your members and not the God who's called you, then you may experience financial hardship because people will no longer pay their tithes or offerings and offer gifts, unlike before. After all, we are all experiencing this crisis unless you are operating from another economy.

All I'm saying is, with the effects of the ongoing coronavirus crisis and war, many would experience personal crises which will eventually have great impacts on their community. Escaping the heinous COVID-19-induced global and personal crises will require a lot of courage, resetting of the mind, and a host of new focused actions; but more importantly, Divine Grace!

Dear friend, I want you to know at this juncture that the purpose of this book is not to scare you, nor is it to report breaking news, feed your fears, or tell you how impossible it is to survive through this season without a scratch. Rather, it is to open you up to the existing problems in the world and proffer some practical tips, techniques, and technologies that have helped me walk through this storm victoriously. Remember, you are a victor, before, during, and after COVID-19 or any crisis.

This book is for you because I didn't just come up with this book. God placed it in my heart while preparing for the new world that's fast approaching. And you will agree with me that scientific and medical experts don't know what to do. They are confused and expecting a miracle from somewhere somehow. All we are asking is for solutions. We don't have to make use of human lives as laboratory rats in a bid to find a cure, vaccine, or solution to this global crisis. So, be informed that this book is not religiously biased, as I believe strongly that at this critical period, we need the collaboration of everyone.

Nonetheless, no matter who or where you are, regardless of your country, race, ethnicity, religion, language, belief system, and conviction, time and **change will affect you**. This is because mankind will continually experience personal, family, community, national, and global challenges, respectively. We can't escape from it! However, you can learn to embrace the changes with a positive attitude and use it to your benefit. This book will show you how.

Therefore, In a quest to know **how change manifests**, I have come to understand that, as long as you're on this planet Earth, you will experience four distinct types of change in life:

- **Change That Happens to Us:** *This is a kind of change that happens to us and affects our personal lives, families, and careers. Truth is, we often can't stop this kind of change because, most times, we didn't create nor anticipate it. It often breaks us and leads to all kinds of changes around us. Good examples are loss of a job, death of a loved one, accident, etc.*

- **Change That Happens Around Us:** *This is a kind of change that comes from a change that happens to us. It affects our immediate society, environment, and nation. This kind of change happens in various forms. It can be from a change that happens to us or in the form of a change that happens in our society and later affects us. A perfect example of this includes hurricanes, tornadoes, storms,* *robberies, floods, and the current global pandemic.*

- **Change That Happens Within Us:** *As an individual, this is a kind of change that happens within us, and affects who we are spiritually, physically, emotionally, and mentally. This kind of change can be positive or negative. Examples of such changes are: purpose discovery, working on our characters or attitudes, changing our fundamental beliefs, depression, etc.*

- **Change We Initiated:** *This often combines the first three changes. It's the kind of change we create or cause to manifest due to our deep thoughts, strategic plans, and untiring actions. I call this 'Catalyst Initiative and Action' (CIA). As humans, God almighty has equipped every one of us to be exemplars of the CIA. All solutions to our earthly problems show up when we commit to this* *phenomenon. Whether consciously or unconsciously, we have at a time initiated something that has either affected us positively or negatively.*

Dr. Myles Munroe of blessed memory once said: "Change is always the introduction of the future to the present. It is tomorrow taking over today, and its denial is a decision to live in yesterday." Eventually, to deny change is to become irrelevant. Simply put, change brings the future to the present and its denial is to keep wallowing in your past while the present and your future are in ruins.

What I am trying to say in essence is that COVID-19 has caused a major shift or change in our lives globally. It has broken the backbone of normalcy and forced us to adopt new and novel methods to run our countries, manage our expenditures, relate with people and most especially how we live, and much more. It has brought the long-anticipated virtual world into the present.

Importantly, it is necessary to remind you that the 21st-century crises e.g., COVID-19 will be the development of a new eon. It would be challenging for those who are not prepared for its arrival, but beneficial to those who anticipated, spotted it, identified their roles in it, proffered solutions, and leveraged it for their successes and significance. These sets of people will become the real heroes, heroines, and leaders of the new world order; because of their ability and capacity to adapt and offer solutions to problems associated with the new world order.

And, in case you don't know, let me amplify and emphasize to your hearing that, the ONLY way to remain relevant no matter what the seasons of life offer you today, is to accept the fact that; as long as you're still breathing and healthy in mind and body, every NEGATIVE thing around you has an expiry date; even the trailer of crises and challenges that COVID-19 and the forces of the Fourth Industrial Revolution brought have their expiry dates!

In other words, everything on planet Earth has an expiry date, including you. Surprised? We are not here to live forever; every one of us has his or her unique expiry date! Thus, your ability to discern, and spot new changes [which might be in the form of a crisis]. This is what will make you a champion and ready to rise over the storm.

Let's take a look at a perfect example that explains the above discourse in my favorite book, the Holy Bible:

"Again, the next day after John stood, and two of his disciples; And looking upon Jesus as he walked, he saith, Behold the Lamb of God! And the two disciples heard him speak, and they followed Jesus. Then Jesus turned, and saw them following, and saith unto them, What seek ye? They said unto him, Rabbi, (which is to say, being interpreted, Master,) where dwellest thou?"

The above story centers on four characters which are: John, two of his disciples, and Jesus. Now, the gist here isn't about the Man, Jesus; but John and his two disciples. What do I mean? The credibility of John's ability to discern, spot, accept, believe, and lead his disciples to the next move of God -- Jesus is one thing. Then, the ability of his disciples to leave their master for another Master is another. In other words, what I'm trying to say is that John and his two disciples accepted the next phase of their life's assignment. They didn't build an empire around the current move they were familiar with – John's ministry. Instead, they welcomed the new move – Jesus' ministry; the new mission and followed the new Master and His mission.

Likewise, don't be stuck in today's success when there are still more heights to attain and greater records to set and break. And always remember, **the greatest enemy of your next success is your last success.** Don't waste time celebrating past victories. Rather, position yourself and keep scouting for the next opportunities in every crisis or change. At this crossroads, I would love us to take a good look at a few examples of systems and structures that have failed to maintain their influence and dominance due to one crisis and another.

Examples and Structures that have failed to Maintain Dominance Due to a Crisis

Let's take a good look at the first world's definition of civilization. And we are going to take a critical look at historical Egypt. This country is known to be the world's power at some point in time. In ancient times, they dominated the world, they conquered and ruled territories across their country's borders, controlling territories like Sudan, Cyprus, Lebanon, Syria, Israel, and Palestine. And the amazing part is that this country is still in existence. According to the International Monetary Fund's World Economic Outlook report, Egypt as a nation was declared as one of the developing countries in the world in October 2018. Interestingly, it is quite obvious that this once continental superpower has lost the power to maintain the domineering influence it once had across different borders in the 21st century!

Let's take a look at the United Kingdom as well. This country is literary called the beginning of civilization. It is a country that extended its dominion and influence over countries like the United States, U.S. (or as it was then the thirteenth colony), the Bahamas, Australia, New Zealand, Pakistan, Egypt, Canada, India, Ghana, South Africa, Sierra Leone, Zimbabwe to mention a few. We must not forget the 'giant of Africa' - Nigeria, too.

In short, the United Kingdom is a good example of the world's true definitions of dominion and political superpower. As a matter of fact, the English Language which is their language is considered to be the world's language. The Internet, for example, is written in English. English is the world's lingua franca. The British Empire dominated the world to the extent that most countries, today, still act and run like the British system E.g., Bahamas Island. But right now, the United Kingdom is not as powerful as before. The Great Britain that controlled the world in the 19th century has ceded global power to the U.S. Its global power status has gone to the dustbin of history, just like the Egyptians, the Ottomans, and the Romans though, they are still relevant in some areas.

To reiterate, countries like Italy, with its almighty Roman Empire, Iran as Persia, and Turkey as Babylon, all have failed to maintain their 'dominion mandate' throughout the ages.

In the business world, NOKIA is another example to be considered. About a decade ago or thereabouts, everyone enjoyed Nokia, its unique products, business culture, and how it operates. They gave their customers the likes of 'The snake game, the soccer game, their ringtones' and all that.

Funny right? But today, in the corporate and mobile phone ecosystem, it has immensely declined. Sadly, it is trying to rise again to prominence in the '5G Race' as data revealed.

But one of the issues that made them fail was their refusal to change. The top managers felt they were at the top in the phone market and as such were untouchable and unconquerable until BLACKBERRY and other smartphones were released in the phone industry and this cost them their highly courted domineering market position. Though they went back to re-strategize, it was just too late for them.

Likewise, the amusing BLACKBERRY with BBM was replaced by WHATSAPP, land phones by mobile phones, you can count on and on. These socio-economic systems and structures are still in existence. In fact, some people still make use of them in some parts of the world today, but the fact remains that they've lost the creative potential and capability to deliver the definition of value the current world desires!

What then is the problem? One of my mentors, Kenneth Soriyan often says "Power doesn't die, it fades. And when it fades, it loses the potency to influence or dominate." So, from the ideas and data I have presented in this chapter, these countries, systems, and organizations have failed to metamorphose into the modern-day equivalent of themselves. And so, they have gone the way of the dinosaurs. They lost the powers and privileges of influencing global affairs. They forgot that as long as they are still on earth, things will keep changing, something will keep expiring and something will keep emerging. This is the reality of existence; nothing remains the same forever!

My life's Anchor (Jesus Christ) made a statement while addressing the teachers and leaders of a group of people known as the Pharisees and Sadducees. He said;

> *"Sometimes the sky is red in the morning and the sky has dark clouds in it. Then you say that today there will be a storm. You can look at the sky. And then you know what weather is coming. But special things are happening now. And you do not understand what they mean."*

He also said to his close disciples when they asked Him when they should expect His second coming;

> *"I will tell you a story about a fig tree. You can learn something from what the tree does. When the new branches on the tree start to grow, the leaves appear. Then you know that the summer is coming soon."*

In other words, we should be able to discern when something special, in this case, COVID-19 and other crises that will arise from it is about to occur. Even if you don't know, you should at least have answers for easy navigation through the change.

A major means the Infinite God can reveal future events or show you the way out is through His Spirit and His Word. However, for these to take place, you must train your spirit to see and hear what He has to say to you. Though He might not give you the full details but trust me, He sure will inform you about it. Remember, you're a spirit man that lives in a physical body. So, you are supposed to know.

Most times, we fail to adhere or give attention to the 'red light' from our spirits because we're so stuck, obsessed with, and sincerely in love with the current tide or trend. We are so obsessed to believe there are no better options until we are caught unawares. A perfect example of an organization that refused to innovate is Yahoo.

In 2005 Yahoo was one of the main players in the online advertising market. But the moment the company loses the ability to see through the season of its existence even when Google and Facebook were offered to them, they missed their opportunity to remain relevant beyond just a mailing company. Their inability to embrace newness and take risks led to their downfall. They failed to optimally maximize the opportunities available for their company in the digital space. They decided to play the old game and refused to innovate.

Conclusively, you should be able to understand the nature or character of a crisis when it is just sprouting its wings. Work to completely understand the nature and character of a crisis. The nature of all crises is CHANGE, combined with a sense of noiselessness. What do I mean? Crises always come in a silent and surreptitious mode. It has an invisible character. You can't separate them; crisis and change. It doesn't make noise at its first stage; it comes as a friend to the prepared ones and as a foe to the unprepared ones. Succinctly, your level of preparation for crises determines its effect on you in its final stage.

CHAPTER **TWO**

Perspective Is Everything

Now that you're very much aware of the kind of changes or crises you should anticipate in this 21st century and centuries ahead, it's of great importance you have the right perspective and attitude towards them. In other words, start building capacities to receive them as they unfold. You can't deny them because denying them will make you unproductive and unprofitable to humankind. Simply put, it positions you as a long-term and lifetime mediocre.

The lens through which we perceive life and experience every bit of its hurdles and successes is majorly based on the mental and spiritual parts of our being. Therefore, the only way to get through difficult times like this global pandemic is to train yourself to see things differently, which is a function of your mental and spiritual capacities.

Interestingly, it's often said that "Life isn't in the abundance of the tangibles but the intangibles." More so, the quality of your life is commensurate to the quality of your mental and spiritual capacities. Since your mental and spiritual capacities are the intangibles that control your life affairs, you need to be mindful of what you see, what you hear, and the thoughts that come to mind. Because humans do better when they see, hear, and think better. This is very important! I would like to add that you develop the powers of 'meta-cognition - the ability to think and rethink the thoughts and feelings that evolve into your consciousness.'

Having said all these, it is key that you understand the concept of crisis, its nature as discussed in Chapter One, its benefits, its purpose, and as well have the right perspective and attitude towards it. In effect, let's take a look at what crisis entails and how it operates.

What is a Crisis?

It has been discussed over decades that, crises have been an integral part of humanity and as well, our personal, domestic, and international experiences and transformation from time immemorial to the present century. However, defining the term 'crisis' is not an easy task because of its ambiguities and interdisciplinary nature.

Although, there is no agreed definition of crisis, yet, different people have shared their thoughts and perceptions about the concept of crisis.

For instance, Coombs and Timothy Coombs define 'crisis' as "The perception of an unpredictable event that threatens important expectancies of stakeholders and can severely impact an individual's and organization's performance which can generate negative outcomes if proper measures are not taken."

In simple terms, this definition highlights the negative impact of a crisis on the effectiveness and efficiency of the affected individual, company, or organization, which can put them in a state of confusion, anxiety, and instability, and above all, underperformance and decline, if not properly handled.

Also, the English defined it as a change for the better or worse.' While Chinese Mandarin defines it as 'danger' and 'opportunity.' But some Western and Chinese Crisis Experts claim that it may mean danger and a 'turning point,' which indicates a sense of the possible positive outcome. How interesting! Context truly matters in terms of interpretation of this phenomenon: CRISIS.

In clear terms, a crisis is an event over which one has no control. It is an experience you did not anticipate or prepare for. It takes you by surprise, and fills you with anxiety, fear, worries, and makes you immobile.

Let's assume the World Health Organization and the world's mental health experts announce that, due to their inability to provide a cure or vaccine for COVID-19, the world must come to a total lockdown for the next 6-9 months. So, everyone is given the privilege to fill their stores with foodstuffs and everything needed. Hence, all activities during this lockdown must be carried out in the digital space, that is: online. What would you do?

Your priorities will change. If you have been planning to visit a friend, I'm sure you will change your plan. If you have a family outside your circle of physical contact, you will keep checking on them to ensure they are safe. You do whatever you have to do to get ready for the lockdown.

My dear, what you just read is an example of an unforeseen crisis that is happening to you and by extension, happening all over the world at the time of writing this timely book. Covid-19 with the lockdown was an unforeseen crisis; no one thought of it or expected it. It seemed like a joke at first, but right now, it's a reality.

Notwithstanding what is happening today, globally, you can train yourself to see opportunities from the ongoing crisis. From the above definitions, I would suppose the Chinese definition is better because it conveys the fact that we can create opportunities out of a situation that threatens us. It reveals that, as long as a crisis can be a threat to an individual, a structure, or a system, it can still be turned around for good if it's well managed.

It is of the truth that a crisis is an event or experience you have no control over. But, let me stress again to you that you can train yourself to turn the event into a milestone of victories in your life! You can choose to prepare for the storm, discern its outcome and plan on how to pull through to stunning success. For example, Eric Yuan, the owner of the Zoom app, is a good example of what I am trying to explain here. He became a billionaire during the ongoing pandemic crisis because people make use of his app as a means of interaction and socialization!

To some people, a crisis is an opportunity while the same crisis appears to be a danger to others. What distinguishes you and the other person is your perspective. You decide which category you belong to based on whatever it is you've fed your mind before the crisis and how far you've prepared for its arrival.

Similarly, others can see what you call a crisis as an opportunity for growth and productivity. What you see as humiliating, the next guy or gal might see as an occasion for the development of humble leadership. It is all in how you see it. It is all in your interpretation, perception, and perspective. The question now is; what is your perspective?

There's this story of a guy I read about in my favorite book. The guy's name is Joseph. He is his dad's favorite because he bore him at his old age. However, his brothers despised him and called him a dreamer because of his 'kind' of dreams. Of a truth, his dreams were odd but had deep interpretations that would later preserve the entire human race in their era. One of his dreams was that he saw the sun, moon, and the twelve stars bow to him. And as a kid, of course, he shared it with the whole family, which made his brothers despise him the more.

Coupled with the ones he's had in the past, his older brothers who happened to be from another mother planned to kill him, but eventually, sold him out to a certain Ishmaelite traveler who was on his way to ancient Egypt. Sadly, the favorite of the father, that's pampered with a silver spoon under his father's roof, suddenly became a commoner in Egypt. This was because the Ishmaelites sold him to one of the top officials of the Egyptian army named - Potiphar.

Interestingly, Potiphar became prosperous and made Joseph the head of his household because he realized that Joseph was the reason for his rising prosperity. Unfortunately, Joseph found himself again in prison because Potiphar's wife lied against him that he wanted to forcefully sleep with her. Despite all these, Joseph wasn't bitter. He knew there were reasons behind his seeming crises and misfortunes. He saw a light at the end of the tunnel. While in prison, the man in charge of the prison soon discovered that Joseph was a good man.

So, he put him in charge of all the other prisoners. Somehow, in the thick of it all, the story revealed to us that: Pharaoh suddenly became angry with his cupbearer and his baker and decided to put them in prison too. Then one particular night, they each had different dreams, but they did not know the meaning of their dreams. The next day Joseph saw how sad their countenances were and he asked them to tell him whatever the problem was. They said, we had a dream, but we've got no interpreter. Then Joseph encouraged them to tell him.

With God's help, Joseph explained the meaning of their dreams. You can check the book of Genesis Chapter 37 to Chapter 50 for more insight about the whole gist of how the cupbearer was released and the baker was executed by Pharaoh, exactly the way Joseph interpreted their dreams.

One night, Pharaoh had two very special dreams, and he was worried and wondered what they meant. The next morning, he called his wise men and asked them to tell him what he had dreamed. But they were not able to tell him the meaning of his dreams.

Abruptly, the cupbearer remembered Joseph and he said to Pharaoh: 'When I was in prison there was a man there who could tell the meaning of dreams.' Pharaoh ordered Joseph to be released from prison right away and he immediately relayed his dreams to Joseph for interpretation. And of course, Joseph interpreted the dreams to be a season of famine and a way out of the global crisis. Happily, he was pleased with his intelligence and ability to give them a solution. Consequently, he chose Joseph to collect the food and store it for preservation. He made Joseph his right-hand man (in a foreign land), I speculate, his vice president. Next to Pharaoh, Joseph became the most significant and powerful man in Egypt.

Eight years later, during the famine, Joseph saw his brothers in Egypt from Canaan. How come? Their father, Jacob, had sent them to Egypt because they were running out of food back at home. In Canaan, famine had swept across the land. Joseph recognized his brothers, but they did not recognize him because he had grown older, and he was dressed flamboyantly. He pretended not to recognize them since they couldn't recognize him too but later revealed his identity to them, which brought about the most shocking news they had ever heard.

His brothers were so surprised that they could not speak. They became so afraid, remembering what they did. They thought Joseph was going to avenge their evil. But Joseph said: 'Please come closer.' When they did, he said: 'I am your brother Joseph, whom you sold into Egypt.' Joseph continued to speak kindly: 'Do not blame yourselves because you sold me here. It was God who sent me to Egypt to save people's lives, through your plans.' He asked for his father and demanded them to go bring his father and every member of the family down to the land of Egypt.

Why am I sharing this fascinating story? PERSPECTIVE! Joseph's perspective was positive all the way. Imagine your brothers or sisters sold you out as a slave to a rich German or Iraq soldier. How would you feel the next time you set your eyes on them as they unknowingly sought help from you because you are now in power? You Know Right?

I would say, Joseph always had this mindset from the beginning. You might ask, how did he come about that? Well, you could see how he welcomed and treated his brothers despite all he'd been through because of their hatred. He forgave them even before he saw them! He set up a dinner party when he met them.

How on Earth is this possible? It's simple! He'd built his spiritual and mental capacity to see his life's experiences or crises as opportunities to be a blessing and a comfort to others; he became a trusted and reliable foreigner in a foreign land. He said to his brothers, "Do not blame yourselves because you sold me here. It was God who sent me to Egypt to save people's lives." He embraced every bit of his crises, stayed connected with his God, and became the savior of the ancient world. He never lost sight of the bright future ahead of him despite all he went through.

You see, this is how people who have trained themselves spiritually and mentally think, speak, and act when they are faced with life's challenges. They count it all joy when they pass through diverse trials! They know the crises are not happening to them, but for them and everyone who'll be connected to them positively.

Though you might not be able to control or foresee the crisis that has hit you because of your insensitivity or because of the nature of the crisis, you can always learn how to control some of your predicaments and problems; you just need the right frame of mind and the 'Joseph-like Perspective' (JP). You can choose to think positively about the circumstances and the crises. You can make some headway against it if you apply (JP). I promise you, that if you do, you will be able to appreciate the crisis because it would force you to change and improve yourself. Hence, let's consider the nature, purpose, and benefits of crises.

The Nature of Crises

Like I said at the tail end of Chapter One, the nature of Crises is CHANGE with a noiseless character. As dangerous as a crisis is, its first stage is as gentle and silent as a dove. With this in view, let's look at the stages of crisis which include; Conception, Incubation, Expression, and Incarnation.

> **Conception Stage**: *This is the first stage of a crisis. It is often called the silent and pre-crisis stage. It's the stage where everything is normal and all hands are on deck. A stage where everyone is trying to avoid any form of*

crisis because it's been anticipated. But on the other hand, if circumstances aren't properly managed, it could lead to the birth of a crisis that might shut a system or person down. It is the warning stage. Most times, what we can't manage or control are the things that later haunt us.

We've seen cases where a doctor wants to develop an antidote to a pathogen or ailment, but later creates a deadly disease that can wipe out the entire universe. Or a particular country decides to develop a defensive weapon against their enemies, but in the process, falls into the wrong hands and becomes a deadly weapon that can destroy nations.

You can say there's always a crisis in every good experience. What makes an experience good or bad is your perspective about it and the ability to control it in the right way before it turns negative. This is often seen among organizations and individuals when it comes to making plans and hitting targets for development. Simply put, at this stage, the crisis is not yet in view. Everyone is fine without knowing the danger ahead.

Incubation Stage: *This is the second stage and it's often called the development or the invisible stage. This is the stage where the crisis exists only in the mind of the ideator, as an idea at that point. It's where the idea moves from the mind to paper. It's where the ideator begins to look out for like-minded folks to support his campaign.*

At this stage, not everyone knows what's up because of its invisible character. The crisis, which is still an idea, is just as harmless as a dove because it is still in the confines of the strategy room. Simply put, the incubation stage is the brooding or planning stage. It is where anything that can become a crisis prepares itself consciously or unconsciously for expression. And of course, nature falls in this category. Hurricanes, whirlwinds, tornadoes, and typhoons, are examples of this stage. For instance, there would have been some movements and activities on the seas and ground that would lead to massive whirlwinds, typhoons, and the likes.

Expression Stage: *This is the third or the implementation stage. It's where the ideator or nature expresses the crisis. It's the stage where the crisis begins to get traction in different mediums, environments, and institutions. The stage where everyone is coming to the awareness of the crisis. The stage where the crisis serves as a means of transmitting hope, opportunities, fear, anxieties, worries, depression, urgency, etc. depending on who disseminates the news.*
It's a season where some sets of people are trying to figure out the validity of

what they've heard or seen, a season where some are already preparing how to protect themselves, their colleagues, organizations, and their neighbors from its consequences, and a season where some set of people are already seeking for opportunities in the crisis. This season often creates panic and makes people restless.

Incarnation/Danger Stage: *This is the last and the most dangerous stage. It's the stage where the crisis becomes viral. It's where the crisis has been verified! It's where it has affected a whole lot of people. This stage is usually the longest, most painful, and sometimes most revealing phase in the crisis's life cycle. It is the stage in which the media are relentless about giving members of the public updates; it's the stage where investigations are launched; a stage where members of the public are assigning blame on* *someone, an institution, or some countries and the like.*

Most times, if it is a marital crisis, the woman might blame the man and the man might blame the woman. In organizations, the low-level management blames the middle-level management and the middle-level management blames the top-level management, this blames the CEO and he or she blames the owner. The owner blames the government and their business-suffocating policies, etc. But if the crisis is a threat to humanity, the people often blame God for allowing it. The funniest part is that they will start having dreams of different scenarios like an angry God, or an angel whatsoever! This was so alarming during COVID.

I must let you know at this juncture that; the victims of every crisis are those who blame someone for the crisis. They are those who look up to external sources for the cause of the crisis. This act is called 'scapegoatism'; it is the act or practice of assigning blame or failure to another, to deflect responsibility away from oneself. All they know is to cast blame; write articles and post them on the internet. Later, they get tired and accept the status quo without taking responsibility for what has happened.

They forget easily that the time of crisis is not the time to blame people. Instead, it's time to take responsibility even though they know nothing about it. Instead of casting blames, change your disposition and carry out your research and learn how to turn the crisis into an opportunity. Like Marie Curie said, "Nothing in life is to be feared; only to be understood."

You see, the moment you take responsibility, you're automatically differentiating yourself from others! What do I mean? Taking responsibility will transit you to the stage of POST-CRISIS. Even though the whole nation or world is affected by the *crisis (like the COVID-19 and the global financial crisis)*, by taking responsibility and making plans, you just got yourself transcended to another realm entirely; and this will of course put you in a vantage position to think up effective solutions in the midst of it all.

As the rest of the world continues to wallow in all crisis characteristics, such as fear, trauma, depression, despair, frustration, anxiety, loneliness, worry, hopelessness, a sense of abandonment, sense of loss, sense of death, an urgency for survival, abuse, crime, domestic violence, and substance abuse, etc., all you have to do is to keep building capacities to come up with new ideas and ingenious insights and solutions. Choose not to approach the same problem or crisis with your existing mindset and ideas. Choose to acquire new skills, knowledge, and new perspectives about the new world; post-crisis. Little wonder, a great mind once said: Crises are the breakfast of champions.

Interestingly enough, one major fact I discovered from observing hurricanes is that they clean things up. The hurricane comes through and creates a mess around the rotten trees, the poor constructions, and the lying dirt around. But five months later, the mess would have been cleaned up. All things would become new! The entire city would look as if nothing had happened. What a fascinating discovery and lesson in 'crisis study!'

The Purpose of Crises

The effect of the fast-spreading pandemic called COVID-19 may be causing many personal crises—or adding to the crises we already have or have been going through before the crisis. Nevertheless, you must understand that there's always a reason behind everything on earth.

The law of cause and effect states that "For every effect, there is a definite cause, likewise for every cause, there is a definite effect". In other words, your thoughts, behaviors, and actions create specific effects that manifest and create your life as you know it. And it's often said that, if you are not happy with the results you are getting from a thing, then you must change the causes that created them in the first place.

On this note, it is important to admit that there's always a reason behind every crisis. So, the purpose or reason behind the crisis tells us what to expect and how we are to respond to it. You can't just ignore a crisis because it's affected a particular area of your life. What you need to do is ask yourself;

"What is going on?" Not "What is happening?"

What is happening will only show you the surface effects of what's going on. It will always make you react instead of respond, which is of course, bad. It is better to respond than to react; responding is taking smart actions; while reacting is synonymous with bad decisions and expressing regrets which falls into what I call 'victimism' or the 'the-why-me-mentality'.

With the question "what's going on?" You'll be able to understand the reason behind the crisis, which will eventually lead you to discern the solution or options suitable for the crisis. It will give room for creative and strategic thinking. It will help you know what to discover, what to stop doing, and what to start doing. This sets and puts you in a vantage position as you adopt the helicopter view to any crisis that crosses your path in life. Trust me, it works!

In a world of 8.5billion people, only a few people have been able to create a virtual and mental space in people's heads. Out of the 8.5billion people in the world today, only a few have created a space for themselves in other people's brains. Think about people like Aliko Dangote, Nelson Mandela, Barrack Obama, Donald Trump, Pastor Richards Osanaiye, Rev. Biodun Fatoyinbo, Bishop David Oyedepo, Dr. Chris Oyakhilome, Bill Gates, Oprah Winfrey, Albert Einstein, Elon Musk, Cristiano Ronaldo, Lionel Messi, etc. The question is: are you part of the people that have created positive and profound real mental estate in other people's minds? Or, are you trying, in your own space, to do so someday? Carefully think about this, please.

If your answer is NO! Then you need to understand the distinguishing factor that differentiates you from those who would answer YES if they were asked the same question. And what could that be? It's simple! They saw a crisis/problem and asked themselves: What solution can my skills, abilities, gifts, or potential and knowledge offer to humanity? How can these abilities and capabilities solve the problem?

Amazingly, if it appears to them that the problem requires new skills and knowledge, they make sure they go through the rigorous process of learning and acquiring the skills or gaining the knowledge so they can solve the problem. Afterward, they master whatever it is and launch it to the world as a solution. This makes them a culture-shaper and a pacesetter. I refer to these calibers of people as the 'Gifts and Glory of the Globe' (3G). This book is a perfect example of creating a mental real estate in your head as you read through it.

Bishop David Abioye of The Living Faith Tabernacle said; *"Every man detests crisis; no one desires or prays to be involved in one. But the benefit of it is that we grow through it."* That's profound, you know! Crises do not necessarily crash people. It rather strengthens if we do not react to them but respond to them. To reiterate what has been said earlier, you can always harness the benefits of a crisis by **responding** appropriately. So, take advantage of the crisis around you even though growth is inconvenient. I assure you, as you do that, people will always place high demand and value on you because you are a solution that will lead them to continuous growth and productivity.

Therefore, let's take a look at the 'Purpose and Benefits of Crisis';

1. **Challenge:** The sole or main purpose of a crisis is to challenge you, your ideologies, convictions, value systems, principles, methods,

and your engagements. It challenges what you've built over months, years, or decades. It allows you the opportunity to question your existence, and as well, reveal how well or how poorly you have managed your resources, your time, and the thoughts that reside in your mental estate before the crisis. And I must tell you; this is one of the moments you need to be sincere with yourself. You need to embrace the challenge. Lock yourself in your room, and go into self-conference, deep reflection, and re-strategize; accept the challenge or crisis and look for ingenious solutions.

What do I mean? Stick to the mission, but always change your methods. Missions and purposes don't change, but methods, strategies, trends, and styles can change. Critically, they should be often changed every 90 days because people keep changing every 30 days into new preferences and prejudices; according to data from sociology, biology, and other related disciplines. Remember, as long as you're on planet Earth, something will keep expiring and new things will keep emerging. This is the immutable law of creation and the Universe.

For instance, communication is a mission but land phones, mobile phones, social media platforms, and the Internet are the methods adopted to carry out the mission of communication. Association is also a mission, but the physical gathering is a major method that's been adopted over hundreds of decades. In contrast with the physical gathering, there's a new normal, which is; virtual realities, online gatherings, intercourses, and meetings. Whether you like it or not, there's a new society that's been birthed because of COVID-19. Hence, you must adjust to the new society.

And for you to thrive, you must accept the challenge. There is a culture shift. In what sense? The world will continue to witness more online meeting and gathering innovations. I think it is going to be a combination of the physical and virtual. Only those who will adapt and learn how the new world would be run will remain relevant. Don't dismiss the things you don't understand; instead, learn how you can adapt and how you can benefit from it. This will not only make you survive but help you remain significant.

You will agree with me that COVID-19 has challenged us to

learn, unlearn, and re-learn. It has brought us to a season of deep thinking and re-evaluation on how humans, structures, and businesses will find their meaning, purpose, significance, and engagement with and without human contact. This is the new order, going forward!

2. **Self-Discovery:** One of the major benefits of crises is self-discovery. As soon as you accept the challenge that comes with a crisis, self-discovery is the first result to observe. You would know your strengths and weaknesses. You would have clarity on what you need to stop doing and what you need to start doing. And if possible, what you need to research and act on to become better. I often tell people that any form of crisis, life trial, and confusion often leads to self-discovery.

Let's take a look at another story from one of the ancient stories of a man named Nehemiah. Nothing is known about his youth or background; but the Bible and history reveal to us that, he was an adult serving in the Persian royal court as the personal cupbearer to King Artaxerxes at a time when the country of Judah in Palestine had been partly repopulated by Jews that were released from exile in Babylon. Though the temple in Jerusalem had been rebuilt, the Jewish community there was still defenseless against their enemies.

So, when the news got to Nehemiah that "Things were not going well for those who returned to the province of Judah and that they were in great trouble and a state of constant attacks and humiliation. The wall of Jerusalem had been torn down, and the gates had been destroyed by fire," He went in, sat down, and wept. He mourned, fasted, and prayed to God for days. The vulnerable and shameful state of the city was enough of a crisis for Nehemiah that he was willing to dedicate years of his life to rebuilding it. But to undertake such a massive and daunting project, he needed the help of hundreds of people, and most importantly, from King Artaxerxes of Babylon.

Fortunately for him, his expertise in the king's court equipped him adequately for the political and physical permutations necessary for the grand project's success. What did he do? He sought help from the king and he was given permission and the resources to rebuild Jerusalem and its structures. He was provided with an escort and with documents that guaranteed the assistance of Persian officials.

So, Nehemiah journeyed to Jerusalem and aroused the people there to the necessity of re-populating the city and rebuilding its walls. Though he encountered hostility from the (non-Jewish) local officials in neighboring districts, yet, he and the Jews were able to finish the rebuilding in the space of 52 days. How remarkable!

You see, Nehemiah's life provides a fine and instructive study of how you can discover yourself via a crisis and as well turn it into an opportunity for leadership and significance. He overcame opposition from internal and external foes. He exercised the administrative and political skills he must have learned from serving king Artaxerxes. His strategy to use half of the people for building, while the other half kept watching for the Samaritans who wanted to attack them under the influence of the infamous Sanballat was just so incredible.

Therefore, it's of supreme importance that you understand his very first step to self-discovery; he reached out to God despite his sorrowful state. That is exactly what you must do. Even though the crisis of life nails and sometimes pins you down, you mustn't give in or give up. Rather, spend some time alone with your Creator and ask for a way out. Ask Him about your role in turning the crisis into an opportunity. There's always an answer. So give it all you can because everything you have experienced before the crisis would be tested during the crisis. Use it to your advantage and discover your real self.

3. **Opportunities:** New and incredible opportunities can emerge from crises if it's viewed from the right perspectives and interpreted with the right frame of mind. By design, crises are meant to question changes in the existing order, in traditional approaches, structures, systems, methods, paradigms, etc. Remember the Chinese definition of crisis; danger and opportunity. So, your perspective which is a function of your spiritual and mental capacity will determine if you can see your crises as an ally to your significance or a foe to your comforting position. Let's take a look at the story of one of Israel's kings in ancient times; King David.

At some point in time, it appears to me that God uses crises to prepare people for what's ahead because He knows the end from the beginning and the beginning from the end; that is why one of His names is: Alpha and Omega. Even though He doesn't orchestrate crises, He surely knows how to make his children know what's coming. He wants them to be like Him; knowing the end from the beginning if they will align themselves to His plans for their lives.

David is known to be the youngest of the seven sons of his father; Jesse. As a young champ who takes care of his father's sheep, he encounters two major crises in his career as a shepherd. While taking care of his father's sheep, a lion and a bear attacked one of the young sheep on two different occasions. However, the amazing part of the story is how he proactively ran after the lion and the bear, attacked them, saved the young sheep from their mouths, and killed them. Amazing feat! Unknowingly to him, this crisis prepared him for what later led to the major victory he had in his lifetime; the fight with Goliath of Gath.

When his time finally came to be recognized, the Philistine army caused a military crisis by engaging the giant, Goliath, to challenge the Israelites to a fight. Everybody was afraid of Goliath. It appeared that nobody was ready to face such a formidable foe. Even King Saul, Israel's leader at that time, couldn't do anything other than to pray for a miracle to happen. Else, the Philistine army will trample them.

Luckily enough for them, their prayers were answered. The young shepherd with the name: David came to their rescue. His father had sent him to bring food to his elder brothers who were parts of the Israeli army. He heard about Goliath's effrontery and challenge, then, he immediately knew that something had to be done. With the combination of his God-given fighting abilities and cleverness, he initiated and devised a solution. He decided to fight the national dreaded Goliath. His brothers saw this as some kind of joke and rebuked him for such foolish audacity just like Joseph's story, which I previously shared.

Fortunately enough, one of the soldiers took him to the king and he explained to the king how God helped him kill a lion and a bear without losing the young sheep in the field. The Israeli king now had an option since no one was ready to risk their lives. Thereafter, the young champ was permitted to try his luck.

Well, you know how it turned out, dear reader. As soon as the formidable and frightening Goliath saw him, he looked at him with contempt and disdain, but David's response to the Philistine was, 'You come against me with sword and spear and javelin, but I come against you in the name of the Lord Almighty, the God of the armies of Israel, whom you have defiled. This day the Lord will hand you over to me, and I'll strike you down and cut off your head. Today I will give the carcasses of the Philistine's army to the birds of the air and the beasts of the earth, and the whole world will know that there is a God in Israel. All those gathered here will know that it is not by sword or spear that the Lord saves; for the battle is the Lord's, and He will give all of you into our hands." What humility and wisdom displayed? What a communicative ingenuity!

David brought out his favorite weapon sling and threw a stone at Goliath's forehead. Bang! It penetrated his forehead and he fell to the ground, confused and surprised. Then David ran over and pulled out Goliath's sword from its sheath to cut off his head. The giant (crisis) had been conquered!

There's a lot to highlight from the above story, but let's stick to the focus. From the first two crises David encountered as a shepherd, he knew that he would be a good warrior if he was given the opportunity. And at last, the opportunity came in the form of a crisis. Though he's been anointed as a king over Israel, he proved himself worthy by discovering the path that would bring him to the palace. He discovered what he should start doing and what he should stop doing (accept the king's offer to remain in his presence and stop being a shepherd). Through the three major crises that led to the beginning of his manifestation, he discovered himself and became significant throughout the decades even till now.

4. **Creativity and Development:** Crisis always forces creativity and development. It creates room for creativity and innovation. It provides powerful motivation for change. It makes you look for new ways to solve old problems. The

concept of neuroplasticity, which is, constant brain changes to form new neural circuits, comes to play when turning your crisis into a storehouse for optimal creativity.

In other words, your brain will expand beyond its default setting for creativity and innovations because of its ability to respond to life's experiences. And failure to respond well to those experiences might affect the functionality of the brain. More so, you need to train yourself on how to make positive meanings out of life experiences and crises. According to Caroline Leaf; life challenges, thoughts, emotions, decisions, actions, and experiences are like trees that can either become a toxic or healthy structure in our brains depending on how we manage them. Hence, we need to be careful about how we perceive and handle everything that comes across our path in life.

It's often said that: leaders tend to grow stronger in crisis but not in good times. They develop and improve more under pressure. Their leadership qualities become sharpened under crises. What this means is that crises place demands on people's unreleased and untapped potentials. When you are under pressure, you will discover areas of your life that you never knew existed. Your ingenuity kicks in. You become industrious and your thinking stretches. You become a creative thinker. This makes crises the cradle of creativity. Because creativity is the same as innovative thinking, you will in the long run discover that the times of crisis and pressure will move you forward into new realms and uncharted territories. Funnily enough, we never innovate when things are working well. We are forced to innovate when something malfunctions - which is exactly what happens in a time of crisis.

Having said all these, it's of supreme importance that you understand that, when I talk about having the right responses and perspectives to a crisis, I am not suggesting that you deny reality. What I meant to say is that you shouldn't let circumstances take advantage of you. You should look for the deeper reality that is hidden in the circumstances. Your response to a thing is controlled and determined by whatever perspective you have.

At this stage, you already know the situation at hand. Covid-19 has happened to individuals and countries across the globe; it is causing great havoc not exempting anyone as you can see. It has destroyed economies, increased the rate of depression, and suicides, globally.

So, doing nothing is not an option. You cannot just sit down and wait for these crises to pass. It is time to stop being a consumer. Rather, start being a creator. Stop being a victim, and start being the one who creates the victories! Don't live with the available choices, start creating options for people to subscribe to. Eradicate the herd mentality and adopt the sovereign individual mentality.

Dear friend, you have got to become the solution you were born to be. You are God's response to a need in the world. You are the answer to a question God knew would be asked in this generation and beyond. You are the fulfillment of one of God's desires. There is something that He wants to do that makes you a necessary part of His plan. Embrace it and I assure you a life of significance.

CHAPTER **THREE**

New World, New Society,

New Normal

To reiterate, COVID-19 has put the entire world in a reset mode. It has allowed us to get ready for the new world. It has given us room to rethink, restrategize, and restructure. It has given opportunities to developing and underdeveloped countries to top up their games in so many areas, especially in the field of technology, health care, education, business, supply chain, and much more. It has also given the entire humankind, be it the developed, developing, and underdeveloped countries massive access to the concept of a world without borders; it has made real and feasible, the act of attracting value, virtual transactions, and influencing lives globally just with a click; and amazingly, it could just happen in your sitting room, bedroom, car, studio, and so on. The world has no walls!

In clear terms, COVID-19 and Post-COVID era is shaping global cultures and they will continue shaping it as a blessing. You might be wondering why I call it a 'blessing'. Yeah! Covid-19 is a blessing in disguise on planet Earth. Even though it wasn't orchestrated by God, I believe strongly that He allowed it to disrupt some of our old thinking, ideologies, ways, and systems. I believe it's a sign to some folks on what's needed to be done in the rapidly evolving new world. I believe it's a call for creative and strategic fore-sighting into the future. What do I mean?

Simply put, it's time for nations, structures, scientists, economists, individuals, and organizations to be creative in projecting the future. They need to be deliberate and creative in carrying out their responsibilities as the future unfolds.

On this note, I have come to challenge you that some of these organizations and systems have leveraged on this new order and are already enjoying the blessedness of the 'Post-COVID Era' while some are still very much ignorant of the new world system. It is not going to be business as usual but it is going to be an era that will birth new ideologies, ideas, convictions, belief systems, values, principles, methods, technological innovations and breakthroughs, relationships, opportunities, etc. in fact, some are birthed already and it is spreading fast.

More so, it is going to be an era of new responsibilities, possibilities, and significance. I see it as an era of redefining moments. Even though the majority has not realized this fact, I am here to offer you a ticket before it's too late. You see, the ticket is for everybody.

But only a few people would eventually journey with us because they are not ready to accept the challenge, build capacities, stretch themselves, and pay the sacrifices required to achieve stunning success and greatness. They are so loyal and stuck to their normal and traditional ways of seeing results.

Planet Earth seems to be in shambles because a lot is going on in different sectors and structures of life. Nevertheless, you should not be idle. You should work out your salvation by getting yourself equipped for what's about to hit the world. Believe me, you need to be ready.

As you can see, a lot has changed to the extent that the term 'Public' has been redefined! Private is now public while the public is now private. We are now so dependent on technology and the internet for our existence; we live and coexist, today, in the cloud or what I call the 'Virtual Planet' and what Author

Neal Stephenson called 'Metaverse' in his 1992 science fiction novel "Snow Crash". The story is no longer the same because your significance and relevance now depend on your acceptance of the new era, the new reality, and the new world.

However, it is important to know that these developments, innovations, and inventions have their negative sides. But the truth is, they are real and they have their positive sides as well. Your responsibility is to learn how it would help you become better in life without losing your sanity, especially as a Christian.

But if you're still part of the majority that thinks the world is still the same or the world would come back to its former state, then you're wrong, or permit me to say, this new world isn't for you. You can either embrace it or you risk being obsolete! There's no room for any form of mediocrity. It is either excellence or nothing. Like someone opined 'Average Is Over!' Even though the new world would naturally bring its negative impacts, you can't just afford to sit back, because its positive impacts would overwhelm its negative side.

I remember one major instruction the Lord gave me while preparing for the year 2020. Friends and close folks in my space at that moment can relate because I shared part of the instruction with them. The Lord spoke to me on the 5th of January 2020 that; "this ten decade (2020-2030) is a moment of redefining moment, assignments, tests, and enthronement. How you spend the first 5 years would determine how you'll end the next 5 years." Though I never knew COVID-19 would bring the world to a temporary halt for all kinds of creativity and innovations; I knew something big was coming but I wasn't so sure what form it would take.

Since COVID-19 is here and has come to stay as some cities and nations are experiencing the 4th wave of its effect, permit me to reiterate the same words in another way to you: Whatever you do between now and 2030 would determine your relevance afterward. You cannot afford to waste this crisis by sitting idle at home. You can't afford to be caught unaware of the increasing trends, fashions, and developments happening in the world. You might not know, but a lot is happening and you need to be updated like never before.

A lot is happening and changing in the world today. Hence, the need to upgrade and reinvent yourself so you can fit in and not be left behind in the new world. You need to know what has changed in the world, what the 'new norms' are, what the new world skills and requirements are, or are going to be, and how you can smartly participate in it, to remain relevant even amid the recession. So, let's take a quick look at how you can upgrade yourself from the aforementioned in this paragraph.

How Do You Upgrade Yourself?

You need to understand that, there's no better way to start than to unlearn some things you've learned before and start relearning from a new perspective entirely. Part of the things you need to unlearn and relearn first is your Identity. Like 1 said in Chapter Two, crisis brings you to a point of self-discovery.

Therefore, for you to have optimal results in self-discovery, you need to unlearn and relearn some things about yourself. You need to know more about yourself. You need to self-evaluate and self-analyze yourself. You need to evaluate your current abilities, expertise, strengths, and weaknesses.

You need to know what has changed about you and what are the necessary new abilities you need to push forward onto success in this new world: 'The Virtual Planet'.

To that effect, you've got to ask yourself questions like:

- *How can I proffer solutions in this current crisis with my gifts, potential, and knowledge?*
- *What are the habits I need to drop that might affect my growth and development?*
- *What are the habits I need to start cultivating for my relevance?*
- *What do I need to know about the new world that would put me in a vantage position for success?*

Answers from these cogent and objective questions will give you clarity on the things you need to unlearn and what you need to relearn about yourself which will eventually make you perform optimally when your service is needed in the global space!

The next phase of unlearning and relearning is to know what has changed in the world. As you're fully aware, the very first thing that's changed in this world in a bid to overcome COVID-19 is man's major medium of communication and interaction with others; the physical gathering. Right now, churches, mosques, schools, organizations, banks, businesses, transportation and tourism industries, etc. are already taking catalyst initiatives to make use of the digital space like never before.

Remote work, remote learning, remote services, and the likes have grown immensely since the pandemic began. The use of technologies and the internet as their major mediums of reaching their audiences and customers and partners, etc. have become their best options. In fact, for churches and mosques, in particular, the use of techs is now their front door tool in reaching their members and congregations while the back door tool is now the physical gathering.

In the business world, another major change we've seen around the globe is the fact that people now do more work at home, exploring digital techs rather than the usual way of doing business. We now have more and more remote workers across the globe doing business. Twitter has even said their employees can work from home forever. Home deliveries are now finding their way right amid this crisis.

Also, customers' behaviors have changed. They don't want to visit stores, supermarkets, mini markets, salons, cafeterias, and so on anymore. People now prefer online transactions to physical transactions. Online banking has now become the most preferable considering the stress. The pandemic crisis has caused a change in our thinking, interaction, and of course, our actions.

I also discovered that their priorities have changed. What seems to be amusing and of great interest before these crises is no longer their interest. They've developed new preferences. Most of them now want to do online business with their smartphones. This has suddenly skyrocketed remote work and increased the 'Gig Economy' (A gig economy is a free market system in which temporary positions are common and organizations hire independent workers for short-term commitments.) players and base. They want to garner new skills like graphic designing, effective communication, and writing, digital marketing, Search Engine Optimization [SEO], data analytics, and many more so they can survive.

Therefore, as an entrepreneur or a marketer, you can't use the same advertising and marketing methods you've been using before the lockdown right now. You need to go digital. However, you need an adequate plan and deliberate effort to be effective because of the vastness of the media space.

Moving forward, before the spread of the coronavirus pandemic, I predicted crude oil would be one of the least resources countries would subscribe to for their economic growth. In a country like Nigeria that depends solely on oil, the Nigerian government must intentionally and deliberately look into other means to sustain the country by diversifying the economy; since the International Monetary Fund has revealed that "Nigeria's economy is expected to shrink by 3.4% and Africa's largest economy could face a recession lasting until 2022."

For this reason, **the world, Nigeria, and most especially, the African countries must know that the greatest resource they can rely on for building a formidable economic system is nothing else than problem-solving and applied or practical knowledge that brings attention and attraction through technology.** If enough resources are driven to the academic institutes and the creative minds in the African nations are supported, then I can ascertain a bright future for us both now and beyond COVID-19.

Emphatically, another change we've seen in the new world is how employment with the use of certificates and MBA degrees would be rated secondary while new skills and technological know-how [especially digital skills] would be primary requirements for employment. Before COVID-19, most organizations in Nigeria and third-world countries depended on employees' certifications rather than their values, problem-solving abilities, and skill sets.

But in this new world, organizations would demand fewer certificates and more personal skills in different areas like technical know-how, auditing, creative writing, digital marketing, leadership, problem-solving, imagination, etc. In other words, there would be high demands for creative and strategic thinkers, problem solvers, and technologists. Though certifications and MBAs will still be relevant in the new world, yet, you must not rely on them because they will lose their capacity to secure a job in the emerging future of work and workplace of the future. You've got to know something the organization doesn't know, and skills they don't have. Or better still, reinvent yourself to get yourself available for the necessary skills demanded by these organizations.

According to the University of Derby, 'The future job market will be looking for graduates with an open mind to explore the unknown future possibilities.'

Having said the above, let's take a quick look into the new normal or trends in the emerging new world. Let's take a peep at the death of small-scale businesses. Since the language of the marketplace has changed since the lockdowns began small and medium enterprises will die because of competition and the newness in corporate culture. Only shrewd and ingenious business owners will thrive in the new post-pandemic economy!

Just like any other person, the first question that comes to mind when a brand advertises a product or service to you in a season like this is: if I patronize this person, what effect would this product or service have on me and my finances? Why should I patronize him and allow him into my space? Will this product or service help me conserve my money or teach me how to multiply my income?

My dear, if you're unable to come up with cogent, concrete, and compelling answers and responses to these questions for your audience through your product or service before you approach them, then you'll get frustrated by their new habits or smart inquiries and wrap up your business.

On this note, you must accept the fact that customers are not the same again. They now have new interests, new access to endless information, and new options. Their behaviors and responses towards things around them have changed. They are now more vulnerable than before. Sadly enough, some of them are victims of Ponzi schemes in this 'bitter' season. But if you're able to make them trust you, then they will pay for your services.

The bottom line is that the majority of the people have lost faith and confidence in the governments, big businesses, and the current systems. They have stopped, actively participating in it. They need something superior and authentic for them to survive through this moment. They need a savior [whether secular or spiritual] to rely on. But for you, you have got to come to the point where you can say, "Every problem has a solution," even though your old solutions are worthless and important at this period. You need a new mindset, upgraded problem-solving capabilities, strategies, and technologies. You have got to embrace yourself because you know you cannot go home and revert to business as usual for survival and significance. The whole world is slipping away from "business as usual."

Nevertheless, do not give up. Do not throw in the towel. Do not quit. Do not take pills. Do not commit suicide. Every single problem has a solution, and it is just within your grasp. This isn't some kind of motivational speaking. It is a reality. You need to stand out for yourself and generations ahead. There's a side of you the world doesn't know yet.

One of my favorite statements and affirmations in my favorite book is this; "You are the light of the world. A city that is set on a hill cannot be hidden. Nor do they light a lamp and put it under a basket, but on a lamp-stand, and it gives light to all who are in the house." In other words, there's something in you and me the world needs for its development. Whether you like it or not, your true identity is to be a light to others who are in darkness. Anything outside this reality means you are a symbol of darkness. But no! That's not who you are. You are a light and you are going to shine. So, in this current crisis, you cannot wait to see what will happen. You cannot leave things up to anyone else. You've got to rise and shine above your limitations.

You have got to release that blessing that is locked on your inside. Don't let fear, anxiety, and bitterness for any system and structure stop you from shining. Let them be the medium through which your light shines to the world. Dear friend, why do you want to be local when your Creator already called you a global citizen? You don't have to limit yourself because you are from Nigeria, the U.S.A, China, Israel, Singapore, South Africa, etc. You need to shine and let the world see your brightness and appreciate God for making you a blessing to the world. If you need to be trained, then, get the training and if it's knowledge in a particular field you need, then go acquire it. You just have to shine and keep shining.

The 21st Century Skills

21st-century skills reflect the idea that the world has changed so drastically in the last few decades. Amazingly, our way of living, culture, learning, education and many others have changed forever. Thanks to the emerging Fourth Industrial Revolution; also referred to as Industry 4.0. This, therefore, brought the need for a new set of skills, new mindsets, new ways, and new values.

What then are 21st-century skills?

The 21st-century skills are a range of competencies, taught across all levels of education, that give individuals the skills they need to navigate their way through an ever-shifting world we're in.

The 21st-century skills transform individuals into "versalitists," that is, people who can apply a depth of skill to ever-changing situations and experiences, so they can gain new competencies, build relationships and assume new roles and responsibilities. More so, these skills, combined with academic or disciplinary knowledge, make one a 'Pluripotent Person'; anyone with the capacity to adapt, adeptly, to any new activity, job, role, or system.

With the way globalization and sophisticated technological advancements are going, changes don't seem to likely slow down shortly. Hence, there is a need for us to be equipped with the right skills and expertise so we can move at the same pace as the world. With the current trade war between the two largest economic superpowers, China and the U.S., I still believe globalization, not the current de-globalization, will become widespread.

With all these in view, students need to prepare themselves for jobs that have not yet been created, technologies that have not yet been invented and problems we don't yet know will arise. Simply put, everyone in this century needs to add some set of values, sterling, and outstanding skills for relevance. Hence, here are some of the lists of 21st-century skills that would be in be in high demand, in the rapidly evolving digital economy:

✔ **Problem Solving:** *this has to do with the ability to determine the source of a problem and then find an effective and acceptable solution. Problem-solving enables you to solve complex problems as they occur. It also involves learning from previous problems, finding new ways to solve existing problems, adapting behavior to different* *environments, and solving problems independently or collectively.*

The concept of problem-solving is in three levels which are; the problem you've seen and experienced, one you've seen and not experienced, then the one you've not seen and not experienced. You see, the highest of it all is the last; the one you've neither seen nor experienced. It commands authority and followership because it would be uniquely tied to you. It's often called the vertical way of thinking. Ergo, this is very important.
To improve this skill, you need to acquire more technical knowledge in your field, be observant, and learn how others solve problems.

✔ **Creative and Critical Thinking:** *creative thinking is a way of looking at problems or situations from a fresh perspective to conceive something new or original. While critical thinking is* *the logical and sequential disciplined process of rationalizing, analyzing, evaluating, and interpreting your creative thoughts or information. Innovations and inventions find their roots in this particular skill. At every point in time, you must have time for creative and critical thinking if you want to be relevant in life. Creative and critical thinking is of supreme importance because they are human abilities. Robots and AI are unlikely to usurp in this new world. This skill makes people compete against their inventions by exploiting the most human of their human qualities. It's been said that there are two types of creative thinking and problem-solving. We have the horizontal and the vertical. Horizontal thinking has to do with creating something from something. It's adding more to what everyone is familiar with.*

For example, creating a social media platform with the same algorithm as WhatsApp is a function of horizontal thinking and it brings the world from something to zero. But when you create something from zero to something, then you've created something vertically. This has to do with creating systems and structures that encourage and create something fresh or new.

✔ **Leadership:** *we are living in a knowledge-driven age where content is king and change is also much more rapid. And because of this, everybody wants to take a leadership role. But on the contrary, my definition of 21st-century leadership is when you are not in charge of groups, organizations, systems, etc., and yet, you're able to make a difference, contribute actively to a community and work in the public sphere to create great influence without being told. You see, if more people accept this role,* *crises will be met with smart leadership at several levels. Leadership vacuums will be less common.*

The 21st-century leader is someone who successfully strengthens their leadership capacity and is highly self-motivated to cause a change. Such a person is hungry to strengthen his or her capacity to both manage and inspire. Most importantly, he exhibits the courage to invite hard truth and work diligently to overcome his blind spots. A kind of leader who respectively looks for options and other ways of doing things. He seeks possibilities of deploying potential around him. He accepts individuals' gifts and potential for a greater course without any sense of insecurity. He doesn't have what I call 'an ownership mindset.'

In other words, all he wants is stewardship. He accepts his follower's failures so they can do better. Finally, he dares to challenge the norms without hesitation in that they re-evaluate their methods and options every 90days. He pauses, ponders, and pursues if he's truly on the right path. But if not, they rethink, reflect, and re-strategize. This is what I call the 'Formula of Leadership Effectiveness', so lacking in our world, and more specifically on our continent: Africa!

✔ **Consulting**: *this is a very special domain. It's an industry for smart, ambitious people. It is for individuals who are capable of analytical, and strategic thinking. They are individuals who are willing to invest a lot of time and energy into brain and cognitive work. It's known to be a people business at its core. Therefore, creativity, leadership, problem-solving, empathy, and social skills play a major role in being a successful consultant. Someone with a variety of methods who makes knowledge actionable.*

Someone who can deal with the complexity of reality. An individual who is well trained in creative and critical thinking.

A 21st-century consultant must be someone who closely watches the world & reflects upon it for opportunities and risks. In other words, the person must act as a futurist. He must be someone who can deal with uncertainties in the future. Mind you, the future is not only about 5 or 10 years. The future has to do with the times and seasons which can be in seconds, minutes, hours, days, weeks, months, and years. Other 21st-century skills you need to be conversant with are: graphics designing, content writing, data analysis, social media analysis, mobile app, and website development, computer programming, etc. So, for anyone to survive and remain significant in this new world, such an individual needs to be skillful in any of these skills but more importantly, hone these 21st-century skills at least.

Dear friend, I must reiterate to you that I haven't written all of these to put you in depression or put you on the run. I wrote it to challenge you the same way it challenged me so you can take responsibility for your future and the future of humankind and generations to come.

✔ **Digital Marketing**: *this is defined as a marketing approach that primarily relies on the internet to connect with the target audience through various digital media channels and platforms. Also, it is an all-encompassing term that consists of digital channels, such as content marketing, SEO, email marketing, social media marketing, mobile marketing, and so on, to create elaborate strategies to reach and connect with prospects and customers. Having said this, marketers and* *different entities will continually make use of digital channels like computers, tablets, and most importantly smartphones, to guide prospects or audience(s) through their purchase journey and keep in touch with their existing customers like never before. It would make marketing easier for entrepreneurs as well as marketers in different structures and organizations.*

✔ **Technological Literacy:** *this refers to one's ability to use, manage, evaluate, and understand technology. It also refers to being familiar with digital information and devices in a modern learning environment. A tech literate is someone who understands what technology is, how it works, how it shapes society, and in turn, how society shapes it.*

Moreover, a technologically literate person can deploy the gift of technology to invent new designs to build things and solve practical problems that are either technological or not. It is also related to media and digital literacy in the sense that, an individual who is technologically or digitally literate is well-versed in thinking critically and communicating with the use of technology. This individual understands how to create, authenticate, share digital content, and can easily adapt to new technologies. Majorly, when an individual is technologically, digitally oriented, and savvy, such a person makes the job faster and more efficient compared to a manual, mundane, or mechanical worker. To be technologically literate simply means the ability to make living easier for the world. It's the ability to know how to marry technology with jobs for effectiveness and productivity.

In a world deluged with both relevant and irrelevant information, clarity is power! With this in mind, it is therefore important to know that you can never overemphasize the importance of clarity of truths in this dispensation of floodlight information. It is a currency everyone is trying to buy with billions of dollars across borders. You have it, you have the world's attention. You don't have it, you wallow into insignificance. Hence, the reason for this book.

The concept of technological literacy or know-how is a currency everyone must-have in the 21st century. It is a kind of gem you discover to sell what you have at hand just to acquire its field. It is a truth that is constantly changing the world so fast in rapid succession. Its movement in changing the world's operations is like that of the speed of light. So for you to catch up with it, you must constantly reinvent yourself and adapt to the concept of Daily Habit of

Learning (DHL); a place where unlearning and relearning take place.

On this note, 'Technological Literacy' encompasses three interdependent dimensions—knowledge, ways of thinking, acting, then, capabilities. Ergo, the goal of technological literacy is to provide people with the necessary tools to participate intelligently and thoughtfully in the world around them. In other words, you must have the right knowledge of what technology is, how to integrate it with your day-to-day life activities, then have the right skill or ability needed to implement them. Even if you don't have it all as an individual, ensure you belong to a community or society that has these three dimensions in place.

However, it is important to note that technology is not only restricted to computers, laptops, software, aircraft, water-treatment plants, and microwave ovens, to name a few. It is more than its tangible products; but about the knowledge and processes needed to create and operate those products, such as engineering know-how and design, manufacturing expertise, and various technical skills like digital marketing, online selling and buying, internet, website management, and development, video streaming, social media like Facebook, WhatsApp, TikTok, YouTube, Ebooks, use of smartphones, blogs, drones, robots, use of computer software like Microsoft and Adobe files, e.g. excel, word processing, PowerPoint, Adobe Photoshop, adobe premiere, etc. Simply put, making use of technology to better your life in all spheres is the bedrock of technological literacy.

Economical New Normal Case Studies

The coronavirus epidemic which swept the whole world at the beginning of 2020 and turned into a widespread nightmare has caused a major economic and social crisis. Governments and policymakers have tried to keep business life afloat with financial incentives, support, and government aids to combat the epidemic. However, the solutions have seemed to be ineffective because the serious contraction of the global economy is massive. In fact, it has put some African nations in shreds of unredeemable loans. Below are two case studies that support the notion above.

Case Study 1

Total external public debt in West Africa as of 2021, by country
(in million U.S. dollars)

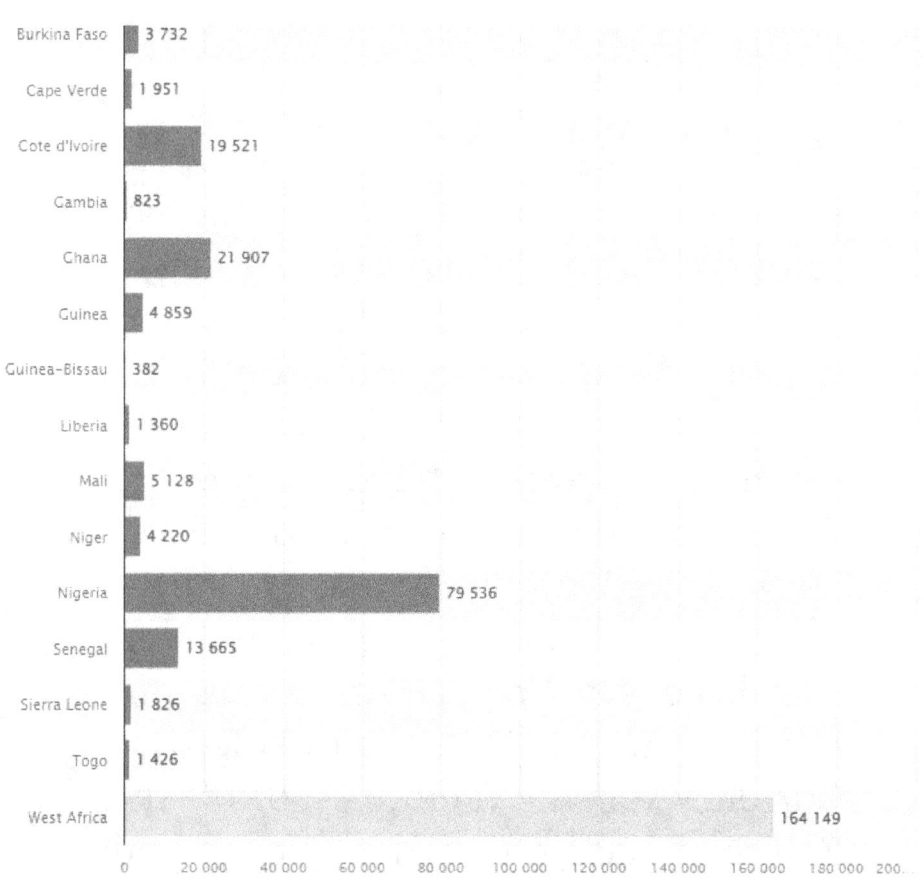

China's response to Uganda's inability to redeem their loan has therefore left the Nigerian government in fear of losing some major assets of the country. According to PUNCH Newspaper, "the total debt owed to the World Bank Group by Nigeria rose by $660m in the first six months of 2022"

Above is an infographic of West African countries currently in debt according to statista.com. And sadly, Nigeria seems to be heading toward the cliff. Assuredly, if all African nations continue to turn a blind eye to the drivers of the new normal ecosystem of business and its operations, we might end up in the era of colonization but in a civilized way. Ergo, all African nations must come to the knowledge of Currency of the Future, Job of the Future, Education of the Future, and Politics of the Future and adapt immediately for them to rise above the tide. These four drivers of the new normal determine the fate of a country. If we choose to be complacent in the middle of this, then, we will doubtlessly glide into irrelevance in grand style.

Case Study 2

It is no longer news that the Uganda government has lost their Ugandian Entebbe International Airport and other assets in the country over the failure to repay a loan.

Uganda's President Yoweri Museveni and China's President Xi Jinping agreed to the release of Ugandian International Airport.

This devastating global pandemic has forced nations and companies across borders to make tough decisions to either shut down their operations or pivot to a new business model or strategy. This has therefore led to Global Economic New Normal; what the business market looks like, how to usher into the new way of working, taking lessons from the past, and deciding what to keep and what to throw out. Since consumers' behavior toward a product, workers' attitudes towards work, sales strategies, and the level of national production and consumption have changed forever, then everyone must embrace this new normal and adapt accordingly.

Realities of the Global Economic New Normal

Taking a critical look at the "new normal" from a business perspective, it is crystal clear that countries and companies will have to adjust according to changing citizen and buyer behavior that was forced by the Covid-19 pandemic and the 4IR. The measures and ideas that have been adopted to prevent and cope with this pandemic will change customers' behavior during and after the epidemic forever. Therefore, having taken a closer look at the wave of the 21st-century crises. Let us consider one major reality that would usher any country into greatness and true dominion as some have been explicitly explained in the pages of this book:

Knowledge-Based Economy

This is a system of production and consumption that is based on Intellectual Capital; the sum of everything everybody in a country, community, or company knows that gives it a competitive edge. It is also the value of a company's employee knowledge, skills, and business training that gives the company a competitive advantage. In particular, a Knowledge-Based Economy refers to the ability to support scientific discoveries, basic and applied research which represents a large component of all economic activities in most developed countries. In this kind of economy, a significant component of value may often consist of intangible assets like the value of its workers' knowledge-how, expertise, or intellectual property.

In addition, the knowledge-based economy both supports, and is fueled by, innovation, research, and rapid technological advancement. The majority of workers in this economy are extremely computer literate and are very skilled at creating business and financial models which will, in turn, lead to data collection, analysis, and the development of algorithms and artificial intelligence (AI) for economical survival.

At this stage, it is important to note that we now have more knowledge-based workers than labor workers in the market space. In fact, ever since Covid-19 forced global workers into remote work, knowledge-based workers became more important than ever before. These workers use analytical, theoretical, or otherwise high-level knowledge to develop services or products, usually online. They often acquire this knowledge through personal certifications on different online platforms especially in most African countries, unlike the developed nations that support this level of knowledge in their educational structures.

Interestingly, it has been discovered that more than ever before in human history, the economy is now dependent on the knowledge factor for growth. To respond positively to these developments and ensure the enhancement of competitive capacities of the national economy, economic policies need to pay attention to knowledge; i.e., innovation and its utilization in all sectors, the new role of technology, entrepreneurship, education, lifelong learning, sharpening the skills of the workforce, and moving from hierarchical to horizontal management structures, along with benefiting from more efficient electronic transactions and communication networks.

As the adage says "Give a man a fish, and you feed him for a day. But teach a man how to fish, and you feed him for a lifetime. Provide him with technology, its know-how, and market linkages, then, you will feed an entire nation." Knowledge, and its application they say, is power. So, individuals, countries, and organizations that want to sustain their relevance and legacy must give room for knowledge and all kinds of expertise in the 21st century.

There is something called the Eight Development Plan that's responsible for the birth of a knowledge-based economy. They include; *starting the implementation of the first five-year plan of the National Science, Technology and Innovation Policy; adopting the National ICT Plan, the National Industrial Strategy, Strategy or Plan for Giftedness, Creativity, and Supporting Innovation; establishing the*

Knowledge Economic City, and the Technology Zone for Industrial Estate and Technology Cities; proceeding with the preparation of a new strategy for higher education, and advancing privatization.

However, there is the ninth and the most important development plan which talks about the adoption of the knowledge-based economy through focusing on education, dissemination of knowledge, paving the way for knowledge transfer, accumulation, its utilization in various economic and social sectors, particularly in production and service activities. Through these endeavors, the Plan seeks to enhance the comparative advantages of the economy, add to the new competitive advantages, diversify it, and increase its productivity and competitiveness, as well as create appropriate employment opportunities for citizens.

The world will be more driven by technology than what we've

experienced before the pandemic. This will either destroy or disrupt the old business model and traditional businesses that are unable to adapt to the changing behaviors of consumers. For example, online teaching or human labor will be replaced by more technology, and robots will directly affect labor and players in various industries. It is a catalyst for those businesses to adapt to the fast-paced world.

Online trading will grow enormously more than what we are currently experiencing as the crisis has forced consumers to change their familiar shopping habits. Technology will directly connect the manufacturer with the end-user. Middlemen will be reduced to an important role but the online marketing and delivery platforms will grow, such as posting info about products on various social media platforms like Facebook, Instagram, WhatsApp, etc.

Conversely, permit me to say on this note that power and authority will no longer be in the hands of some world-leading nations or kingdoms of this dispensation anymore. Instead, it would be wielded by individuals and corporations that have mastered the arts or dynamics of power and attention engineering. In other words, those who own data, and algorithms, and can get the world's attention would be the world powers. Simply put, they will own the future.

These sets of people are considered to be rich, talented, skillful, intelligent, and innovative. They have the ability to get the masses addicted to whatever product they produce. They determine the affairs of life and tell you how you ought to live your life. They monitor you and everything that goes on in your life; both internal and external.

Dangerous right? Yeah! And that is why you need to brace up and reinvent yourself.

Coupled with the rise and rapid advancement in the field of bioengineering and AI, there would be a massive separation of humankind into a small class of superhuman(s) and a massive underclass of useless masses. The future of the masses will then depend on the goodwill of a small elite because the masses have failed to expose themselves to what the elites are exposing themselves to. For example, the movie titled "SQUID GAME" is a perfect example of how the elites would have total control of the masses.

Succinctly put, the masses would trade their freedom of life for survival because the flow or circulation of resources, especially money would only be monopolized by the elites. Sadly, it has started!

Therefore, the purpose of this book is to bring you to the knowledge of these realities so you can be a part of **SmartNation**, an initiation designed for you and all African nations to help us build a legacy and leverage the technologies introduced by the Fourth Industrial Revolution and implement them on a national scale. A structure designed for proffering smart solutions for organizations and systems.

This initiative aims at increasing total factor productivity, improving the lives of all African citizens, training, raising, retaining local talents, and attracting foreign talents. We focus on building smart cities that empower citizens, support businesses, and inspire community innovation. Smart new and creative solutions that ensure the City operates more efficiently, attracts and encourages businesses, and improve the overall quality of life.

The Future of Education in the 21st Century & Beyond

Sir Ken Robinson said and I quote "The more complex the world becomes, the more creative we need to be to meet its challenges." Innovation and technological advances are constantly changing the ways we communicate, work, and live together. Education systems that reflect this dynamic will be most capable of responding effectively to the current and changing needs of young people, society, and indeed the labor market. Hence, the need for us to creatively adjust to the new realities that have befallen planet earth.

Of a truth, technology has affected our lives one way or the other. It has also improved many sectors. However, education remains one of the key sectors that have and would benefit more as technology continues to grow. With cheap broadband and improved infrastructure, among others, there is a high possibility that education will become more accessible and simpler for students and teachers. But for us to optimally maximize this astounding reality, the education system of African nations needs to gear up its games. What do I mean?

Why go to school when you could learn the same information faster by watching a Youtube video or playing a computer game? Why memorize facts for a test when you have all the information in the palm of your hand anyway? Teachers, lecturers, heads of schools, and educational institutions need to know that past methods make little sense to today's students who learn and think differently. The truth schools are failing to teach students to respond to rapid change and how to handle new information because they are clinging to obsolete methods.

Ergo, this is a call to every educationist out there to help the students of the 21st Century explore their creativeness and ingenuities. They need to know that 21st-century students are not a bunch of students sitting quietly at desks, in neat rows, writing down every word that the teacher says or writes on the blackboard (or smart board). Instead, they are students who want a new academic syllabus to stay relevant in the future market space.

For instance, the **World Economic Forum** predicts that technology could displace 75 million jobs by 2022, but will also, in turn, create 133 million new ones that might make the unprepared masses unemployable.

The question now is, how can we prepare ourselves and our children for a world of such unprecedented transformations and radical uncertainties? How can our syllabus (especially in Africa) make them employable in the future job markets? Will they fit into the new world order of the technology-based world? Mind you, I am not talking about the ability to make use of social media via their smartphones. Rather, the ability to reinvent themselves for the possibilities in the virtual planet, proffer solutions to global problems and lead the global landscape of technical know-how.

Critically, a baby born today will be in his thirties by 2050. If all goes well, that baby will still be around in 2100 and might even be an active citizen of the 22nd century. As a teacher or parent, what will you teach that baby that will help him or her survive and flourish in the world of 2050 or the 22nd century? What kind of skills will you equip him or her with in order to get a job, understand what is happening around him or her, and navigate the maze of life? Can he or she compete with the students of the advanced countries?

On this note, the role of the 21st Century teachers and heads of schools should be to help every student learn how to learn. It should inspire creativity, encourage collaboration, expect and reward critical thinking, and teach the students not only how to communicate, but also the power of effective communication. These are skills students need in order to thrive in today's and tomorrow's dynamic workplace. They need to know, understand and operate in what I called 'Intelligent Networking' which is; emotional intelligence, mental intelligence, physical intelligence, social intelligence, and executive leadership management, and open them to the world of scientific possibilities to make life better and easy to live because the world is no longer the same. It has changed and it's in a progressive change. Permit me to say, **_the world is scientific._**

If we want to provide every student with a 21st-century education, we must foster deeper learning through the purposeful integration of rigorous academic content with experiences that intentionally cultivate in them the skills, mindsets, and literacies needed for students to become lifelong learners and contributors in our ever-changing world.

This kind of education responds to the economical, technological, and societal shifts that are happening at an ever-increasing pace. It's an education that sets children up to succeed in a world where more than half of the jobs they'll eventually function in don't even exist yet. In short, it's an education that provides students with the skills and competencies they need to thrive in the 21st century and beyond.

It is therefore important to note that 'education for the 21st Century and beyond' recognizes the fact that we are living through a period of rapid change in an increasingly globalized environment, which requires the adaptation of the education systems, not just through a one-off reform, but continuously.

With this in view, there must be a reformation of the curriculum. Why? The curriculum framework can set the vision for 21st Century education and as well, guide the learning objectives and outcomes expected of all students in the country. The process of curriculum reformation should therefore define the knowledge, skills, attitudes, and values young people will need to thrive in the world, not just today, but in the years to come.

This process should be evidence-informed, taking into account global research and experience on competencies as well as national aspirations and development goals. It should also be consultative, drawing on the voices of young people about the skills they need as well as the learning approaches which are most relevant to them because not everyone is the same way. For instance, some students learn via reading alone. Some learn by hearing words, looking at pictures, watching a movie, watching a demonstration, or participating in a discussion which can all be categorized into; Verbal Receiving, Visual Receiving, Receiving & Participating, and then doing – a passive and active way of learning.

Having said this, teachers must be helped to understand the new competency-based approach and must have access to good resources and guidance to help transform their classrooms into platforms where students can apply their learning and engage in more collaborative activities such as project-based learning, research, analysis, and problem-solving tasks. Without this, learning in the 21st century would be impossible.

So, before it's too late to catch up with the trend of the 21st Century, I implore all educationists and heads of schools to take their students via the new route of learning. Else, our existence as a nation and contributor to the world's advancement would be insignificant.

Let's **Brace Up!**

CHAPTER **FOUR**

Generation Lockdown and the Virtual Planet

In this Chapter, we would be looking at the various definitions of the term 'Generation', its theoretical concept, the types, and as well, considering how they have constituted the development of planet Earth.

The Cambridge English Dictionary defines the term 'generation' as all the people of about the same age within a society or within a particular family, or the usual period from a person's birth to the birth of his or her children: the last or next generation.

However, the theoretical aspect of the above concept by 'Karl Mannheim' in 1928 points out that people that have similar values, behaviors, and living styles were born in the same time interval and if possible, the same mindset, global environment, culture, and lifestyle.

On the other hand, the concept of the term *generation* has two basic meanings. The first concept has to do with a familial lineage or generation while the second concept has to do with a social generation, that is, a set of people born in the same date range with the same life experiences. In the sociological use of the concept, a *generation* consists of a group of people who are born within a limited time range and share not only the same date of birth but also similar socio-cultural values and life experiences.

Simply put, a generation is a group of people born around the same time and raised around the same place (or not) but with similar life experiences. These sets of people exhibit similar characteristics, preferences, communication, values, and motivational preferences because they experienced similar trends at approximately the same life stage and through similar channels like games, sports, music, fashion, religion, online games, TV, smartphone, and the Internet, etc.

As a matter of fact, the differences in geographical locations, experiences, and life events across the globe make it difficult to have a definite consensus on the definitions and types of generations. So, the variances in years of birth, geography, and the likes make us have varying physical characteristics, or what the biologists call phenotypes (refers to the observable physical properties of an organism; these include the organism's appearance, development, and behavior. An organism's phenotype is determined by its genotype, which is the set of genes the organism carries, as well as by environmental influences upon these genes.), in different parts of the world.

Strauss and Howe, two authors who have written extensively on the subject, employ the following divisions that have been adopted in this book:

- **The Silent Generation**: *these sets of people were born between 1927 and 1946. These sets of individuals were born during 'World War II'. They are called the silents or the traditionalists because they were raised during a period of war, economic depression, and acute hunger. They tend to be in their 60s, 70s, and even 80s in today's world. Most of them are retired, but those that are still working seem to be largely aging partners, managers, or senior support staff. They prefer to take simple information which is clear and can be summarized like direct mail or written communication because of their old age and life experiences. This* *generation is considered to be hardworking because of their resilient attitudes to survive through World War II. It's been noted that they are the ones who brought a strong work ethic to the workplace.*

- **The Baby Boomers**: *these sets of people were born between 1943 and 1960. They were born in the aftermath of the Second World War. They tend to be in the age range of 55, the 60s, and 73. They are the generation that first rejected many traditional values of previous generations of population increase with different strategies of childbirth reduction. They're currently between 56 - 76 years old. Members of this generation believe in the importance of hard work and working long hours with the mindset of long-term employment. Though their parents had fought in the war, all they wanted was peace, equality, and a desire for change. They are known to* *be great optimists, whose passion for modernity culminated in the birth of new music and fashion styles. Younger Baby Boomers were the first generation to spend their incomes lavishly because of the invention of credit cards in developed countries. While those in the underdeveloped and developing countries are preparing themselves for their country's independence from the colonial masters. In the same vein, these sets of people were able to afford a more lavish lifestyle than generations before. They have the mindset of giving their children the best education because most of them were not privileged.*

- **Generation X:** *these sets of people were born between 1961 and 1981. They are called post-boomers. They are in the age range of 39, the 40s, and 54. These sets of people seek better career opportunities which led to the evolution of the 'Electronic Age' and* *widespread usage of technologies. They have high sensitivity towards social events; have high motivation for business and success. Since this generation was mostly brought up by workaholic parents, they could solve their problems independently. The sale of the first personal computer happened in this generation and this seemed to form the infrastructure of changing the technology habits of the generation. Also, a common characteristic of Gen X is their comfort level with computers, smartphones, laptops, tablets, and other technologies employed in the dynamic workplace. They tend to be less committed to a single employer and as a result, are more willing to change jobs to get ahead in life than previous generations. Having seen the lifestyles of generations ahead of them, they have this mindset and ability to manage different jobs together in a bid to cater for their families.*

- **Generation Y or the Millennial:** *the term 'Millennial' generally refers to the generation of people born between the early 1980s and 1900s. They are between the ages of 23 and 38. It's a generation that has to work for a living. In their lives, technology is the symbol of many things. They are basically entrepreneurs. This generation is considered not to like work, but the fact is they work whenever they want to and do more entertainment and leisure-driven activities. They act aggressively and assertively, consume fast, have dissatisfied manners, and seek independence. Their most important characteristics are freedom and the use of technology. They are mostly in the shackles of technology and loneliness. They are known to be "online 24 hours." They are the first generation to grow up with computers and digital media under the age of five. They have* *access to their friends, families, information, and entertainment every moment of the day. One other characteristic of this generation is self-confidence which makes them undertake multiple missions. Also, they can make advanced thinking and innovation. They have the will and strength to welcome change and are always ready to follow new approaches. They are highly entrepreneurial, creative, and not risk-averse.*

- **Generation Z**: *These set of people are born between 1995 and 2019. They are often called the internet kids or 'the digital generation. They are called the true digital natives because, from their earliest moments on planet Earth, they have been exposed to the internet, social networks and mobile systems which make them have little or no memory of the world as it existed before smartphones. The average Gen*

Z received their first mobile phone at the age of 10 and 13 years. Many of them grew up playing with their parents' computers or laptops, and mobile phones or tablets. They have grown up in a hyper-connected world that's made smartphones their preferred method of learning and communication which often makes them spend, daily, a minimum of 5 hours a day on their mobile devices. It was observed that over 50% of them have not entered any bank for the past 3 months because of the use of mobile banking apps which are on their mobile phones. Also, these sets of people are knowledge-driven, more restless, smart, and more inquisitive than the previous generations. Limitless access to world-class information, knowledge, and data makes them super intelligent!

Having said all these, researchers have shown that the concept of a generation has different birth years and lengths according to different historians and scholars because of several factors like family backgrounds, personal convictions, environmental values, life experiences or activities, and many more. For instance, if you grew up in an urban, wealthy, educated, and freedom-loving environment, certainly, your life's experiences, outlook, and how you interpret life would be different compared to someone who's raised in a rural or poor background.

A perfect example is seen in the storyline of some Israeli students aged between 13 and 15. When one of their instructors asked if the students are interested in starting their own companies in the future, the response they received was blank and unbelieving. Why? They replied indignantly, "What do you mean by 'in the future?' We have started our own companies! "The future you are talking about is now! We're already projecting and designing a better future for our business." Can you imagine? Sounds unbelievable right? Hence, this is one of the reasons why Israel is referred to as a 'Start-Up Nation.' Its citizens' capacity to establish world-class and profitable businesses.

In this age, this is the type of one-second embarrassment every innovator prays for. It's the type of mindset that Bill Gates, Elon Musk, Yuval Noah Harari, Caroline Leaf, Oprah Winfrey, Mark Zuckerberg, Jeff Bezos, Warren Buffet, Aliko Dangote, Mike Adenuga, Strive Masiyiwa, Folorunso Alakija, etc., have.

You see, the above story shows how smart and prepared they are even before their youthful life. However, in some third-world countries, things are different. An average 18-year-old student is still confused about purpose and vision in life. Most of them have no clue about what's happening in the world. They are clouded with so many wrongs and the saddening part is that the educational systems in these climes are not helping matters! They need reorientation and new leadership with the fervor and determination and above all, insight, required to reshape and remold the existing cultures, consciousness, and minds of their peoples. The earlier this is embarked upon, the better.

It's Generation Lockdown!

My definition of generation in this book has nothing to do with age but has a lot to do with our socio-cultural life experiences, even though your generation is of the traditionalists, the baby boomers, the millennials, the X, Y, and of course the Z. No doubt, it is the combination of different generations that are presently going through the coronavirus crisis; though it is experienced in different geographical locations and with different responses. Countries like China, South Korea, Germany, and of course, Nigeria are all affected, but today, observed data shows that they all responded differently.

I coined the term 'generation lockdown' from the recent crisis, globally referred to as COVID-19. As you're very much aware, COVID-19 is the abbreviation for 'Coronavirus disease 2019'. It's an infectious disease caused by a newly discovered coronavirus. The World Health Organization (WHO) says that "Most people infected with the COVID-19 virus will experience a mild-moderate respiratory illness and recover without requiring special treatment. However, older people and those with underlying medical problems like cardiovascular disease, diabetes, chronic respiratory disease, and cancer are more likely to develop serious illness from the disease."

On this note, the World Health Organization (WHO) concludes that the best way to prevent and slow down the transmission of this deadly disease is to protect oneself and others from infection by using a face mask, staying indoors, washing our hands frequently, and not touching our face. This, amid other health-related factors, encouraged world leaders and health managers to call for a worldwide lockdown; either temporary or permanent.

What then is Generation Lockdown?

Generation Lockdown is used to describe a group of people who live in different geographical locations, experiencing a crisis that's common to all. In other words, *generation lockdown has to do with the coexistence of all generations with the same crisis on the same planet but with different responses*. It's a generation that enables individuals to spend quality time with their families. A season that brings back what's most lacking in various relationships, families, friendships, and other human-centered attributes and eccentricities.

Generation lockdown serves as a reset button for most people. It's a season that allows parents to get familiarized with their children and children get to know their parents. It's a season that's instilled the value of looking out for each other. A season where people are more united and strongly bonded like never before; a very unusual season where the world, its elements, and components came to a consensus on a particular issue; and I am convinced this moment would be one of the most unforgettable moments in the history of the world. Even the unborn generations would have to be told about this global incident because of its uniqueness.

Also, this season has been a season of all kinds of discoveries and commitment. It's a season of restructuring and re-evaluating one's life. A season of self-reflection and intense evaluation on how life should be spent. It is a period of reflecting on how life ought to have been spent before the lockdown, during the lockdown, and how it should be after the lockdown. Significantly, this season should be a season of unlearning and relearning; a season of capacity building for the post-COVID-19 era and its uncertainties. Consequently, it will lead to a season where the underdog will undergo various training in readiness for the emerging virtual world of the 21st century; a season that will give more room for collaborative efforts in different organizations, structures, systems, countries, and institutions.

Interestingly, some people have found themselves busier than ever, especially during the lockdown and post-lockdown. Juggling the technological challenges of working from home with the new job of unlearning and relearning. It might seem difficult at first but in the long run, people will adapt and start building their lives around it. A fact that attests to one of the social science's beliefs is that: "man's ability to adapt to a new environment and new routine can shape his character and personality whether he knows it or not."

As I've said earlier, it is valid that COVID-19 has its negative impact, but trust me, it's also a blessing in disguise. And some people would certainly look back in the post-COVID-19 era and appreciate 'the COVID-19 moments' because it happened to be their season of rediscovery, refining, re-strategizing, and re-launching onto fortune and significance.

It is an incontestable fact that: survival is the first level of intelligence in any kind of crisis. Therefore, it's very important you know that we won't be in this state forever because planet Earth can't contain the blessedness of eternity. It lacks the potential to make anything on earth last forever. Since the current earth is not eternal in its current state, it can't and will never be able to make anything or any human [especially if it is negative!] maintain its absolute dominion.

Generation lockdown may be long, but it is not forever. By the time the "long" runs out, some things will have changed. It may be you; it may be your crisis itself; it may be both. But you must bear in mind that your personal crisis or this global crisis is only for a season.

Another way to put it is by reminding you of the aphorism that says: nothing is permanent except GOD and His promises of a good and peaceful plan which is a better future. That all things will work together for you because He loves you. No matter what you're going through, or what you have been through, during the lockdown. I am here to tell you humbly that: you will always see His goodness and mercies if you believe and have faith in Him!

That seasonal change, goodness, and future are some of His most consistent ways of bringing hope to you. This means that you should not throw your hope away, even in the darkest season of COVID-19. Generation lockdown will end and it will consequently usher you into a new world and a new blissful order. You must be ready for that world. You must be equipped for your effectiveness and efficiency. You have got to close out one chapter to open up the next one. And this is how it works; most of the time, you have to get ready for a level that is bigger and better than the one before. So, the seed you've planted in generation lockdown will determine your harvest in the next generation I called; 'The Virtual Planet.'

The **Virtual Planet** (VP)

The year 2020, I have no doubt; will always be remembered as the year that changed the course of human history forever because of the effects of the global pandemic. And that one major effect is the fact that; COVID-19 has shrunk planet Earth's future into the present - a future where everyone lives virtually. More so, a future where technology and a more fascinating online presence, will increasingly be parts of our lives and corporate existence.

A future where smart and sophisticated technologies have become inanimate members of the family; a future that can't thrive without the use of technological systems and devices. A future that makes most engagements like business deals, travels, meetings, voting, lectures, and many virtual. And as a Christian with the Wisdom of God at work in me, I believe this is one of the signs we should consider for the greatest crisis that will hit the world in the future. Let those that have ears hear what the Spirit of the Lord is saying at this moment.

Of a truth, it is not that humankind has never come across crises or radical and bitter transformations before. In fact, the whole of human history is full of stories of crises and how the crises have contributed massively to the major transformation like building monumental architectures and cities in Egypt, Babylon, Italy, Jerusalem,

Western Asia known as - the pre-pottery Neolithic, etc. and these are even seen in some parts of the world today.

Afterward, the world moved to the first industrial revolution which helped advanced civilizations and spread Christianity in most of the African countries. It also led to the evolution of modernization and political ideologies like communism, capitalism, democracy, and concepts like human rights, freedom of the press, higher education, entertainment craze, etc. In other words, the entire human transformation is founded upon the factor of time --- the distinguishing factor between the present and the future, which makes me believe that the future you seek is in you if only you know the best time to birth it.

However, in the history of humanity, the year 2020 serves as a season for another remarkable shift with the presence of the deadly disease: Coronavirus that birthed more sophisticated crises. And the surprising part is how the news of its heinous havoc spreads faster on various media platforms, especially the virtual/digital than the virus itself. As it rides on the wings of different virtual media platforms, mankind will also ride on the wings of the virtual media channels to keep themselves and their loved ones ready for what is ahead after the first stage and last stage of COVID.

With the ongoing global pandemic, the rapid transformation we are experiencing in this season is solely built on the new planet we've designed for our survival and significance; "The Virtual Planet' (VP). Tools and technologies of the virtual world, or the virtual planet as I call it, all came to the human rescue! A VP is an environment or a world that is advanced, regulated, and managed by technologists and their technologies. Though this experience has been in existence before now, Covid became a tool of its massive explosion and acceptance.

A planet that makes communications, interactions, and all sorts of life's activities exist in the virtual space with the aid of virtual applications, systems, devices, technologies, etc. A planet that births a world of online tech-savvy that synchronizes the online communities and the offline communities.

With the ever-changing world and technological advancements, planet Earth would experience a dimension of newness that's never been witnessed before even though the year 2020 had been predicted to be a season that will lead humankind into unimaginable breakthroughs, innovations, and growth.

An example of this technological transformation is the concept of

'Tele-presence'. 'Tele' simply means distant; therefore, 'telepresence' is the virtual or digital ability to appear at some distant or far away location without the biological components (Physical entities) of an individual or group. Virtual technologies such as virtual and augmented realities sometimes provide unique telepresence experiences.

For example, you can be in Nigeria and at the same time be virtually present in China, the United States of America, or anywhere in the world. It also refers to a set of technologies that allow a person feels as if he or she is present and as well, helps give the appearance of being present at a place other than their true physical location.

While some educational institutions, for example; Nexford University, NobelHouse College Abeokuta, Premiere Academy Lugbe Abuja, and some others are clearly at the forefront of leveraging this new environment and experience. In the next 2 - 5 years the world will see a dramatic shift in the number of students taking classes online versus the traditional classrooms. In other words, schools would become technology-driven organizations that use technologies for learning and pedagogical purposes.

Before this crisis, the majority of the human population was already practicing a scientific term known as 'Parallel Universe;' that is, doing two different things at the same time in two different places. Succinctly put, you could be here and now, and at the same time be in the cloud or the VP (Virtual Planet) explained earlier.

Also, **it is the idea of someone who exists in two dimensions doing two different things at the same time**. For example, a man can be addressing his staff in his office and at the same time making his wife who's at home smile or laugh uncontrollably. Or having a physical identity and having another identity on different virtual platforms like Facebook, Instagram, Snapchat, WhatsApp, Twitter, and metaverse to name a few.

Nevertheless, all of our virtual experiences are still dependent on our physical gatherings, interactions, and transactions. In other words, we still have the choice to either dive into the virtual planet's realities that are just unfolding or we keep on clinging to our traditional ways of life - physical association.

As a matter of fact, in less than 2 months, the earliest moments of generation lockdown changed the equation. The lockdowns made human beings do away with the previous lifestyles they were accustomed to for thousands and thousands of years and suddenly adopted COVID-19's forced ways, and culture! Physical gatherings and engagements were put on a hold. Everything stood still for the callous pandemic: COVID-19!

We began to witness how almost every individual, institution, system, structure, or country started to migrate to the virtual planet to cope, adapt, and at least stay abreast of key activities in their various industries. This became the compelling doorway to the new normal. In other words, human beings started looking past the norms of how they lived, dressed, worked, communicated, practiced religion, worshiped, learned, sought health care, and entertained themselves. All things are becoming new in the evolving Virtual Planet!

Sometimes last year during the 3rd wave of covid-19, the United States of America had one of the greatest virtual club parties on Instagram that recorded 100,000 viewers and attendees. Can you imagine? It's been recorded that the hottest party in town as of the 2nd wave of covid-19 was that of DJ D-Nice's party on Instagram and it attracted celebrities like Rihanna, Oprah Winfrey, Will Smith, not excluding Mark Zuckerberg and Mitchell Obama to mention a few. Can I be sincere with you?

This is just the beginning of a new norm, a new culture, and a new way of life. Even though the lockdown has been eased, the majority would still prefer online engagements. You'll hear statements like, "if we could sign business deals on zoom successfully, then is there a need for us to fly down to your country to sign this? If we could enjoy the virtual club party during the lockdown, do we need a physical gathering to make one?

Amazingly, just like millions of people watched the singer; Ariana Grande virtually performed at Fortnite, the popular Canadian Justin Bieber also hosted an interactive virtual experience on the 18th and 19th of November 2021. According to the press release, it was said that "Bieber's virtual event will offer fans a futuristic look into the metaverse, merging gaming, real-time motion, and live musical performance into an immersive interactive experience."

The **Metaverse**

Just like we switch on our data to connect with people across borders through different social media platforms, and websites on the internet, we are going to adopt the concept of metaverse to connect with people globally. Amazingly, we will not just connect with the universe. We will connect *to* and *with* the internet

The word 'Metaverse' is a combination of two words. 'Meta' and 'Universe.'

Meta means 'beyond' and 'verse' is taken off from the universe. In other words, it means something that is beyond our current universe. One can also say that it is a concept that describes the future of the internet as we see it today. It is also described as a place between the real and the virtual for people to come and collaborate whilst finding value in the activities they do.

It is a world that fuses different digital technologies such as social networks, virtual or augmented reality, and video conferencing with users immersing themselves in its digital environment where they can interact as avatars. In this metaverse world, you will be able to transact using NFTs or cryptocurrencies. You could buy a car or a virtual piece of land. You could build a stadium to host a concert or build an art gallery to showcase your giftings and get paid with metaverse currency (which many have considered; the future of money). It is a world that gives room for a double lifestyle on the virtual planet.

However, it is important to note at this junction that there is nothing valuable about a Dollar, Euro, stone, coin, or any tangible money in the world. The only reason these currencies are valued is that we all decided how invaluable they are consciously or unconsciously. Money, therefore, is a collective story or fiction we tell each other about its exchange value. In other words, the elites determine the value of everything in this world including money. They set the agenda and decide the global economic flow till it becomes acceptable to the masses.

As priceless as the tangible currencies are in this world, the elites and some part of the world population have decided to change their medium of transactions by inventing other streams of transactions like Bitcoin, Ethereum, Dogecoin, Litecoin, Tron, NFT (Non-Fungible Token), etc. These currencies are therefore considered to be the money or currencies of the future.

Currency **of the Future**

As a result of the Fourth Industrial Revolution (FIR) and advancements in technology, boundaries between digital and physical transactions have also changed forever. In other words, the financial world is no longer the same. Even though we have all kinds of cryptocurrencies in the world right now, you must be reminded that the internet space is quantum in nature. That is, it is wide.

Therefore, you never can tell which of the cryptos can be the dominant currency of the future. As I said, the elites would be the ones to determine which crypto would rule the crypto world. For a while, it is bitcoin, some said Ethereum, but right now, we have NFT; Non-Fungible Token (An NFT is a digital asset that represents real-world objects like art, music, in-game items, and videos. They are bought and sold online, frequently with cryptocurrency).

NFT has been projected to be the currency of the future. But the truth is, NFT will not always be the currency of the future. Someone somewhere is working on something greater. Hence, the reason for my previous assertion which says the only reason some currency would be valued is because of the value we place on them. So, your responsibility is to get informed daily. Don't just be a consumer of whatever is being decided, rather, be part of the decision-makers in your world and be the difference.

On this note, permit me to say, there is no getting back to the pre-covid19 world. There is only moving forward.

As the world keeps changing, we also need to change in some positive ways so we won't be left behind. So, see through the changes from the pages of this book and ensure you find your place in it.

Hence, everyone that wants to move from survival mode to significance mode in this season must accept the fact that COVID-19 will reset planet Earth largely into the 'virtual reality mode'. A mode of operation that makes people want to work from home like never before. Simply put, the new world order will now become a virtual reality world.

A year from now, the world we will live in will be very different. In actuality, it will impact how we live, how we work, interact, and how we use technology. Almost everyone who wants to thrive will need to be tech and digital savvy; people who use technology to drive or foster what they do, be it in churches, restaurants, banks, corporate firms, governmental organizations, schools, and systems.

With this in view, I have come to believe that what affects a single person anywhere will affect everyone everywhere because we're quantumly entangled together. The digital age has made this strange phenomenon of quantum physics a broad daylight reality in the 21st century. So this is one of the moments we need to think and act in unison rather than worrying about race, ethnicity, nationality, religion, social or financial status, etc. We need to learn from the past, project into the future, and make our present pleasant as we continue to live in this new world. It's the best time we all need to come together and create systems and structures for the coming Age. It's time to introduce yourself to yourself and be the catalyst to your world.

Distraction **Management**

Fortunately, now that people can do nearly anything on their personal digital spaces which will, of course, increase dramatically in the next 2 - 5 years, you must know what is called "Distraction Management' (The act of having control over your decisions to avoid distractions of any sort. It is the act of exuding enough discipline to combat distractions on your path to fulfillment)" amid these new norms, habits, behaviors, and ways.

As an individual, organization, corporate firm, systems, and structure, you must accept the fact that there's enough content in the digital space to distract you off course if you're not careful and disciplined enough. This increasingly emerging digital culture will be extended to the education ecosystems; it is called 'Smart Education.' Students will be able to use their devices for a multitude of class and non-class-related purposes. And if proper measures are not taken to overcome the over-reliance on these techs and devices, it might in the long run derail the purpose of education; especially 'Education 4.0' which is needed for the workplace of the future.

Education 4.0 is the desired approach to learning that aligns itself with the emerging fourth industrial revolution – (The Fourth Industrial Revolution is described as the advent of "cyber-physical systems" involving entirely new capabilities for people and machines. While these capabilities are reliant on the technologies and infrastructure of the Third Industrial Revolution (Electronics, IT, and Automated Production), the Fourth Industrial Revolution represents entirely new ways in which technology becomes embedded within societies and even our human bodies.

Examples include genome editing, new forms of machine intelligence, breakthrough materials, and approaches to governance that rely on cryptographic methods such as the blockchain). In other words, 'Education 4.0' is a school of thought that encourages non-traditional thinking when it comes to imparting education. It uses technology-based tools and resources to drive education in non-traditional ways.

Therefore, since the industrial revolution focuses on smart technology, artificial intelligence, and robotics; all of which now impact our everyday lives, different learning institutions like secondary schools or high schools and universities will have to start teaching and continuously keep teaching the students about 'Smart Education' as part of their curriculums. Also, changing the approach to learning altogether, and utilizing this opportunity to better improve the students' chance of surviving and remaining significant on the virtual planet.

On this note, let's take a look into the few ways to manage distractions in the emerging 'Fourth Industrial Revolution' or what the Germans call 'Industry 4.0:

- Set your priorities right
- Break them into objectives and targets with a deadline
- Tag your mobile data for a purpose
- Design leisure time for yourself
- Have the habit of DHL (Daily Habit of Learning) – ensure you have a goal to learn something new about the relevant skills in demand on the virtual planet.
- Mute or freeze any app that might distract you
- Take some time out
- Then make sure your priority is something worth fighting for.

With your adherence to the aforementioned, you will be able to manage your engagements online and offline, constructively, and more importantly, beneficially.

Having looked at this current crisis from a helicopter and positive mind, it's imperative you understand that, since the world is in a recession, and this does not seem to end anytime soon; global opportunities have shrunk. Most affected are 2020 graduate students across the world. The market, customers' behaviors, preferences, and prejudices have changed in the sense that what they used to gravitate towards has changed in this period because necessary measures to contain the virus have led to an economic downturn in so many countries, especially in the African countries like Nigeria. As a result, people are working from home and stepping out only to buy the essentials. Moreover, consumers have drastically reduced their spending because of job insecurity and post-COVID-19 effects.

Honestly speaking, I have come to understand from my informal research that when a country is in a recession, the members of the public and especially, the consumers stop participating in the business world because they want to conserve their income to survive. They stop buying things. And the effect is that: when buyers stop buying, the sellers will have to stop producing; jobs will start disappearing because companies and businesses will stop investing and recruiting. And if this happens, income will dwindle; citizens will be impoverished and start looking for alternatives. Only those who have envisaged a season like this and planned will be the only ones in the market.

As these continue, the level of crime and human degradation across the country would appreciate drastically. It will penetrate homes and create an atmosphere of discord in families which will later escalate into disputes between spouses and different groups of people in the larger societies.

Before you know it, fear, trauma, depression, despair, frustration, anxiety, loneliness, boredom, worry, cluelessness, hopelessness, urgency for survival, abuse, and then crime would become the order of the day. And I must be sincere here; this is exactly what is happening around the world; as reports and data all show. Frankly speaking, you might not be experiencing this in your space. But know that, the fact that it's not happening in your space doesn't mean it isn't happening in other locations, geographies, and countries, respectively.

If you take a serious look at the world today, you'll realize that the world is experiencing an economic depression that is caused by several mass depressions in different countries. And if this continues, countries, especially African nations will be paralyzed, dispirited and so desperate to survive. And the moment a country is in this state, the citizens will begin to despair and they may consider suicide or protests as the only option left. This, if not curtailed, may escalate into a national crisis. Think about the famous 'Arab Spring' that began in Tunisia or the recent 'Black Life Matters' in America.

Moreover, some of them will begin to look for different means to earn money, which of course might be in illicit ways. In a bid to survive, different people would brand foolishness as wisdom and mediocrity as excellence because they've got no option left but to resort to illegal means for survival. And if proper measures are not taken by the government, the power centers of that country might take laws into their hands by making the citizens depend solely on them for survival. What a calamity!

Afterward, personal crises like domestic violence, divorce, murder, robbery, etc. will increase, which will eventually make people insecure even in their own homes. People will become afraid. They will lock their doors and guard what they have left. They will feel threatened and start defending themselves, sometimes with violence. It is the 'end of the world' they'll say!

However, my admonition to you, dear reader, is: that you do not have to become sucked into the storm. Even if your whole nation is in a crisis and there is nothing you can do about your circumstances, you have one thing left;

take responsibility for yourself and your family legally.

You might ask, "Sam, how do I take legal responsibility when the language of the world has turned to the survival of the fittest?" Well, I want you to know that there are some people in this world earning daily legally. But before they could get to that point in their lives, they considered the following, which I will like to honestly share with you at this juncture:

- **Pause**: *the world is in a state of interregnum. And the most critical part is that you must also come to this state if you want to survive. You need to stop running and toiling. Some might have adopted the idea of survival of the fittest, but you don't have to. You can do better than that. This is the moment you need to be sincere with yourself and your current* *position. At this trying moment, you need to go to your **'invironment'** or inner circle and your 'personal' war room. At this moment, you need to pay more attention to yourself. Then, admit you're helpless and accept the fact that you need help. You see, there are three types of people in this world; people that don't know they need help, people that know they need help, and finally, people who think everyone is the reason for their problem; they fail to take responsibility and they are not seeking help. Mind you, agreeing to the fact that you need help isn't a sign of weakness as many have believed. Rather, it's a profound strength and a creative move to getting out of your current predicament. Everyone must come to this stage in their lives if they want to be relevant in life.*

- ***Superior Power**: as you reach out for help, you must understand that not everyone can help you. Not all pastors,* *coaches, consultants, professionals, and experts can help you. So, before you open up to anyone, ensure the person is spiritually, mentally, physically, and emotionally mature. Ensure the person is not in the same mess as you. Ensure the person is accessible and ready to help you even if you're at fault. Most importantly, understand that the best `Person' in the right position that can help you is God. Hence, make His Presence your critical war or strategy room in this season. Whether the people of the earth know it or not, what they need is outside help because this crisis has beaten the wisest, richest, and strongest of our species! And the fact is that deep inside of us, we know we cannot solve this crisis by human means. The nature of man yearns for something superior and powerful to human nature and that's why we are so captivated with 'superman' and other superhero stories. Superman was born in Krypton according to the* *comic book and he came to earth with superpower abilities; he uses his superpowers to help and save people who are in all kinds of crises because he's above them. And according to my favorite book, a verse says, "He that's from above is above all including crisis (emphasis mine)." So the help we need isn't right here on our planet, it's from above. Therefore, the help you also need isn't here. It's from God. As you position yourself right in His presence and seek His face, I assure you, that He will show you which way to go and what role you need to play not only for your survival and significance but also for the world. You don't need many answers; you only need just one answer from Him to solve this crisis and others in the future.*

At this juncture, why don't you drop this book now, take some time out and ask Him to help you? Tell Him how much you want to have a personal relationship with Him. Let Him know how sorry you are to have subscribed to other means of help outside Him. Tell Him how much you want to abide in Him forever. Tell Him you're ready to wait in His Presence until He instructs your heart. Tell Him to give you the grace to make your heart fixed on Him. Tell Him to make His Will and Solution yours, Amen.

Conclusively, as you carefully take responsibility for your life and the lives of those around you by seeking help from Him, ensure you document everything and each process He shares with you. Then, convert them into principles for action and share them with others because the world needs saviors, messiahs, and superheroes like you. You can't afford to miss this part. It is a very critical resource for your life's significance!

CHAPTER **FIVE**

Final Significant Admonition

Hello Dear, I'm glad to announce to you that we're in the last chapter of this book. And in this chapter, we will be forecasting, projecting, and predicting one of the greatest events or crises the world should expect in decades to come. Together, we would consider its nature, and how it's going to affect the entire world both the elites and the masses, except those who have been preparing their whole life for it.

For instance, COVID-19 is a blessing to those that have been preparing themselves for any kind of crisis. To some, it is an eye-opener and a sign of something amazingly coming their way. But to others, it is a curse – perspectives! if only we can discern the times and seasons of life. If only we can tell what has happened and what's yet to happen.

The same will be the effects of this forthcoming crisis mankind should expect. The truth of the matter is, that we've all been living with this crisis all our lives. While some are busy preparing themselves for it, some are wasting their resources on the intangibles that will make them victims of the crisis. This crisis, I tell you, is a journey to another experience entirely in the history of humankind.

Theoretical physicists, scientists, and futurists like Professor Michio Kaku once opined in a bid to proffer solutions to future crises and unforeseen events with the statement; *"trillions of years from now, the universe will be extremely cold. We think the universe is heading for a big freeze. All the stars will blink out and will cease to twinkle. The universe will become so big and cold. And at this point, all intelligent beings in the universe must die. The law of physics offers a death warrant to all intelligent lives. Therefore, there is only one way to escape the death of the universe; it's to leave the universe. Though we're now entering the realm of science fiction. But at least we now have equations of a strange theory that will allow us to calculate if it's possible to go through a wormhole (a hypothetical connection between widely separated regions of space-time.) to go to another universe where it is warmer and perhaps start the human race all over again."*

But as a bonafide student of the Bible and with the help of the Holy Spirit, I have come to understand mankind cannot escape from the forthcoming crisis. The death of the universe the physicists are trying to escape from by relocating to another planet or universe be it mars won't come to reality because of the nature of the crisis. The forthcoming crisis would ride on technology's back; especially when it hits its highest degree of performance and intelligence. It will occur when the world is fully informational, digitalized, hyper-connected, technologically affluent, and sophisticated. It would be a season where famines, pestilences, and wars, would appreciate and the love of many would wax colder. A season where everyone is relaxed and enjoying themselves without the consciousness of what's coming ahead.

Moreover, there would be technological unemployment because humanoids and robots will begin to play a major role in businesses, schools, institutions, structures, governmental decisions, etc. They will become part of the family; carrying out various activities that will eventually lead to a reduction in the world's population because of advances in medicine, genetic engineering, longevity, birth control, and the likes.

Also, the concept of 'transhumanism' would be introduced to merge human consciousness with that of an AI machine. Critically, some cities would naturally be populated by this kind of species. Military personnel, scientists, and medical staff would be the first to take advantage of these, especially when war arises. This aforementioned concept would ease the pains of the amputated soldiers, regulate blood pressure, repair some organs due to aging, accelerate the healing of wounds, and many more medical miracles. For example, Prof. David Sinclair of Harvard is at the forefront of the *'Human Longevity Project'*, while Prof. Jennifer Doudna, co-inventor of CRISPR Cas9 is helping to end any form of disease in the human body.

However, amid all these events and trends, the Church would have learned how to effectively engage the use of technology to preach the Gospel of

Christ. Technology would be a massive effective instrument in their hands for disseminating the teachings of Christ. The Spirit of God would have His full course on earth, God would be glorified, souls would be immensely won, the Body of Christ would experience the greatest manifestations of the Spirit of God, and the Gospel of Christ would be preached all over the world.

Then, suddenly, the major crisis that I have been talking about would hit planet Earth, and there would be a massive disappearance on planet Earth. This disappearance won't be a function of escapism to Mars or any other universe or multiverse, like what Tesla, Amazon, other CEOs, etc. postulated and are planning and investing billions of dollars into presently. It won't be a function of death. Rather, it would be the much-anticipated spiritual event, phenomenon, and glorious exit of the Church, known as '**The Rapture**, which the Holy Bible spoke about in clear terms, two thousand years ago after the ascension of Jesus Christ.

Some scientists on earth by that time would eventually believe in the existence of God and not dark energy. They would see no need to evacuate planet earth to mars or the multiverse again because that evacuation would have happened. So, in the real sense of it, they are right. The earth needs to be evacuated but not the way they've planned or imagined it.

Brothers would leave their sisters and sisters would leave their brothers. Husbands would leave their wives and wives would leave their husbands. Christians and every other person who believes in Jesus Christ and have been gifted with the Life of God would disappear from planet Earth.

Afterward, the whole world would be in chaos, and confusion, "for then shall be great tribulation, such that never exist since the beginning of the world to this time, nor ever shall be;" says the Bible. During this period, the smartest, wisest, and strongest of men would be clueless about what to do.

The global power centers of the world would have no solution because they would be caught up in the shock as well. Some will have to rise to the position of authority to ease the tension, fear, desperation, grief, and despair in their country. Then, a world leader would arise to instill peace and unity on Earth to no avail. The concept of 'global citizen' would be fully practiced. He would try his best, but to no avail, because this event – rapture would lead to all sorts of crises that would continue for 7 years.

There would be scarcity and a global economic downturn. Life on planet earth would be called survival of the fittest. To survive, you have to belong to a fraternity that is ruled by the antichrist; a group of people(s) from different parts of the world that will provide all you need but in the end make it impossible for you to be saved when Jesus comes back the second time for the people who reject and disobeys the doctrine and lifestyles of the fraternity. Then, Jesus Christ and the glorified Church; (those who disappeared) will appear in the sky to give judgment. The question now is, which one is better, to believe in Jesus right now and be raptured when He comes or rejects Him now and fight for your salvation for 7 years with tribulations and torments from agents of the antichrist? You decide. Nevertheless, I would admonish you to choose LIFE by believing Him and be saved NOW!

My dear, I must reiterate, that this book isn't a book of doom. It's an eye-opener to the whole world and to those who are ready to listen to what will happen to our temporal habitation: earth or what I call the 'Virtual Planet' in this instructive book. You see, schools have done their best by giving us certificates, degrees, and preparing us for job opportunities. Education on the other hand has done its best by making the world more pleasant to live in with all kinds of transformation. But the peak of enlightenment the world would behold soon will be called 'Revelation – Spiritual Intelligence (The ability to connect to God and have a conscious relationship with Him)'

Revelation, on the other hand, is what is given to whoever that's connected to Jesus; the Revealer. He's revealed these things to me and I'm glad to be His mouthpiece in a time like this. This revelation should also prepare you for a brighter world after the 21st Century Crises. Take responsibility and see to it that you're not left behind. Ensure you're more connected to God so you can reign eternally with Him. That should be the cynosure of your entire existence!

Conclusively, I want you to know that crises are always going to be part of the equation of life on earth until the coming of the Messiah; Jesus Christ. The following questions are for you:

1. *Are you well equipped for the virtual planet or you are about to start preparing yourself?*
2. *Do you think you have what it takes to bring peace and tranquility to your world with your gifts, potential, and the instructions you've received from God?*
3. *Will you be prepared for the next global crisis called the rapture in decades to come?*

After reading this book, you should see the need to believe and accept Jesus

Christ as your Lord and Savior so you can be saved, kindly repeat these words with me;

"Father in the name of Jesus, thank you for sending your Son into this world to die for my sins. I believe He is the Way, Truth, and Life. I believe and accept Him as my Lord and Savior. I renounce the world and accept the Gift of Salvation as I receive the Holy Spirit. Thank You for making me brand new. Hallelujah."

If you genuinely say the above prayers, then you are born again and born into the family of God. What you need right now is to join a Bible-believing Church where you can be taught the way of the Lord. Remember, you are no longer the former person that picked up this book. You are entirely new! So, live worthy of your new life and shine brightly in your world.

Conclusion

This book is an eye-opener and a book of instructions for the next six months and decades ahead. I want you to keep beholding it alongside the Bible to discern the seasons of your life on planet Earth. I leave with you the peace of God that surpasses all knowledge and understanding. Amen!

I Celebrate **You.**

Summary

One of the major setbacks most African Nations, government parastatals, organizations, and entrepreneurs have faced in a bid to stay relevant in the 21st century is their inability to predict the future by wallowing in the present success and forgetting to plan for the future with a vision. They choose to stick to their old methods and strategies of getting things done by not adapting to the ever-changing world. But having forecasted into the future, I saw the need to contribute to the success and development of many organizations and businesses in this ever-changing world full of surprises. Therefore, this book is the answer to the questions most of us have not sat down to ask ourselves in a bid to get things done. It is a book designed to help you forecast the future of your BRAND, PERSONALITY, and as well, help you survive and remain significant in any form of unforeseen crisis. Whether the crisis is self-induced or externally motivated, strategies and ideas that would help you rebound and shine are documented for you in this book. This book is written to help you prepare well for the current and future crises by conserving the resources you have (especially money), multiply them, and as well, adequately prepare you for the new demands and skills in the digital market space. I assure you, that with this book, your future is secured!

About the **Author**

Samuel Adeosun is a purpose-driven futurist who discovered purpose and his core assignment early in life. He is a full-time pastor in the Glorious Liberty Church, Gbokoniyi Onikolobo Abeokuta, Ogun State, under the leadership of Pastor Richards & Gracious Osanaiye.

He has been called and ordained to raise and train exceptional leaders from different professions and fields of life. Aside from being a full-time pastor, Samuel with his spiritual insight has learned how to successfully merge and balance his life's calling with his career without faults. Therefore, this has created a zeal in him to pioneer a movement called **SmartNation** – an initiative that aims at empowering citizens, supporting businesses, and inspiring smart and intellectual community innovations. It focuses on smart, new, and creative solutions that ensure every citizen operates more efficiently, and employable to improve their overall quality of life.

Samuel is the author of 3 books titled; Roadmap to Purpose Discovery, UnMasked; Unveiling the Spirituality and Science of Your Uniqueness, and Create Your Online Course.

Samuel has consulted for organizations like Premiere Academy Lugbe Abuja as a corp member, Sultanah Royale, Waka Logistics, Bucris Empire, and Kaina's Wardrobe in New York and New Jersey. He has also, trained and released leaders into different structures and systems in order to make a difference with their God-given potential.